HAUNTED
ABERDEEN
& DISTRICT

HAUNTED ABERDEEN & DISTRICT

Geoff Holder

Black spirits and white,
Red spirits and grey,
Mingle, mingle, mingle,
Ye that mingle may.

William Shakespeare, *Macbeth*

First published 2010

The History Press
The Mill, Brimscombe Port
Stroud, Gloucestershire, GL5 2QG
www.thehistorypress.co.uk

Reprinted 2010, 2011

British Library Cataloguing in Publication Data.
A catalogue record for this book is available from the British Library.

ISBN 978 0 7524 5533 4
Typesetting and origination by The History Press
Printed and bound in Great Britain by
Marston Book Services Limited, Didcot

CONTENTS

ACKNOWLEDGEMENTS

One of the pleasures of writing a book such as this is that the author gets to include a roll of honour for the fine people who have contributed to its production. Firstly, I owe a debt of gratitude to Rachael Hayward and Al Hayes of East of Scotland Paranormal (ESP) for actually making this book possible. Secondly, thanks go out to all the people who put up with my impertinent questions and let me poke around their premises – with a particular tip of the stovepipe hat to Diane Melville and the staff of Reptiles in The Green; Craig 'Flash' Adams and the staff of the Moorings Bar; Chris Croly of The Tolbooth Museum; Paul Hudson and Johanna Duncan of His Majesty's Theatre; John Dow and Robin Bradford, Centre Manager and Security Manager respectively of Aberdeen Central Market; and the staff of the Old Blackfriars.

I am also grateful to the staff of various museums, institutions and other organisations who politely and efficiently answered my sometimes bizarre queries. Respect is due to those writers who have gone before me in this area, particularly Norman Adams and Graeme Milne, both authors of fine books on the supernatural in the North-East. The staff of the AK Bell Library in Perth and Aberdeen Central Library were unfailingly helpful. And, of course, there is the divine Ségolène Dupuy. Just because.

This book is part of a larger grouping of works by this author dedicated to the mysterious and paranormal. For more information, or to contribute your own experience, visit www.geoffholder.co.uk.

INTRODUCTION

What indeed do we not owe to the influence of the departed?
They are not dead. Thousands of them live for us, they still speak to us out of every century,
and from far down the ages, till we have reached the furthest bounds of history.
Somehow they seem all around us.

Henry Montgomery, *Life's Journey* (1916)

In many respects the departed are indeed all around us in Aberdeen, for in some ways it can be seen as a city built on the dead. People have been living on the thrust of dry land between the Rivers Dee and Don for thousands of years, and prehistoric burials have been uncovered in many places, from King Street to Schoolhill and Mounthooly. The area around The Green – now covered by Carmelite and Stirling Streets, among others – was the site of several extensive medieval cemeteries. More built-over graveyards were located at Correction Wynd and Gallowgate. Hundreds of skeletons have been found beneath St Nicholas Kirk. There were plague burials near York Street, while executed criminals were interred where they were hanged, at Gallows Hill near Pittodrie and the former East Prison (now the site of the headquarters of Grampian police). Hundreds of people died violently at the Battle of The Green (1336), the Battle of Craibstone (1571) and the Battle of Justice Mills (1644).

Of course, the view that ghosts are the spirits of the dead, although popular, is only one hypothesis among many. Throughout this book you will find people who subscribe to various psychic, spiritualist, religious, psychological, scientific and magical beliefs about ghosts. These views may be contradictory or complementary, but their sheer diversity shows that the subject of ghosts is not easily solved by one approach – which is why phenomena that baffled and alarmed our ancestors continue to fascinate us today.

Despite extensive (and often unsympathetic) urban redevelopment, Aberdeen is fortunate in still possessing some wonderful historic buildings, such as the sixteenth-century Provost Skene's House and the seventeenth-century Tolbooth, both of which are open to the public and allegedly haunted. These are covered in the first chapter, 'The Historic Centre', which also includes many other allegedly haunted locations – from libraries and theatres to shops and street corners – in the heart of the city. One challenge to the standard view of 'ghosts as the spirits of the dead' can be found in the cases examined in Chapter Two, 'Poltergeist!' A broader range of phenomena flourishes in the private homes haunted in Chapter Three, 'There's a Ghost in My House' – as early as the 1500s Aberdonian writers were recording that some houses were haunted, a tradition that continues unabated today. Ghosts of academic and student life – not to mention some truly spooky paranormal events – make up the following chapter, 'Old Aberdeen', the home of the University of Aberdeen.

Pubs, hotels and other buildings open to the public for the price of a drink or a meal are detailed in the chapter entitled 'Spirits Served Here' – this section probably contains the most extreme contemporary phenomena in the book. Chapter Six, 'All Aboard!' introduces a miscellany of ghosts who have travelled by bus, tram, truck or train. And finally, we conclude with cases of supernatural soldiers and other creepy tales from the countryside in the chapter on 'Phantom Armies & Rural Terrors'.

The cases described in the book draw on many earlier published sources such as books, articles, periodicals and newspapers (plus YouTube!), supplemented by new research conducted in 2009-10. Some witnesses who shared their stories with me asked to remain anonymous, while others were happy for their names to appear in the book. I am grateful to them all. Any mistakes in transcription or misinterpretation are of course my own. A list of allegedly haunted locations open to the public can be found in the Appendix, while the key published sources are listed in the Bibliography.

Welcome to Haunted Aberdeen. Enjoy your stay, and please ignore the faint traces of ectoplasm.

Geoff Holder, 2010

one

THE HISTORIC CENTRE

From medieval times up until the late 1700s, Aberdeen was essentially a small patch of irregular streets and crowded buildings bounded by Castlehill to the east, the valley of the Denburn to the west (where the railway and dual carriageway now runs), the River Dee to the south (now diverted and re-engineered as the docks area) and a reedy loch to the north. The Castlegate was the very centre of the burgh, the main road north to the Bridge of Don leaving by Broad Street and Gallowgate, and the only route south a twisting inconvenient switchback following Shiprow, The Green, and then the Hardgate to the Bridge of Dee. The topography was dominated by St Katharine's Hill, which was levelled when Union Street was built, straight as a die for a mile, in 1801. The straight lines of Marischal Street, Union Street and King Street have been superimposed on top of the original street plan, but the medieval pattern can still be made out in the older streets, particularly where the ground slopes down from the higher ground beneath Union Street and towards the shoreline. This means that central Aberdeen is a split-level urbanscape, with an 'underground city' of underpasses, culverts, cellars and tunnels passing beneath the 'flyover' of Union Street.

Punishment and the paranormal at the Tolbooth

At the centre of the old town was the Tolbooth, the centre of civic administration, tax-gathering and justice. Much of the original building has been replaced, but Aberdeen is fortunate indeed to retain the former Wardhouse or prison, built between 1616 and 1629. Now called the Tolbooth Museum, it is situated off Castlegate between the Sheriff Court and Lodge Walk. It consists of a number of eighteenth-century cells containing displays relating the civic history of Aberdeen, with particular emphasis on crime and punishment.

As well as countless ordinary felons, the prison was used to house people accused of witchcraft, rebel Jacobites, and Quakers who were persecuted for their religious beliefs. Many condemned criminals, including numerous murderers, spent their last nights on Earth here, sometimes unable to sleep for the sound of the gallows being built outside in readiness for the hanging.

With this history of violence, suffering and death, it is not surprising that the Tolbooth has come to be regarded as haunted. Indeed, with its narrow spiral staircases, original doors, chains

Right *Aberdeen in 1661. The River Dee almost laps onto The Green, and St Katherine's Hill dominates the tiny town. (Author's Collection)*

Left *Aberdeen in 1822. Union Street and other straight routes have been imposed over the medieval street pattern. (Author's Collection)*

Below *The small town of Aberdeen in the seventeenth century. The spire in the centre is St Nicholas Kirk, with the Tolbooth to its right. (Author's Collection)*

Clockwise from above

The Tolbooth as it was in the early nineteenth century. (Author's Collection)

Lodge Walk, the alleyway beside the Tolbooth. (Author's Collection)

The Tolbooth in 1661, at the heart of the city, surrounded by the space of Castlegate. (Author's Collection)

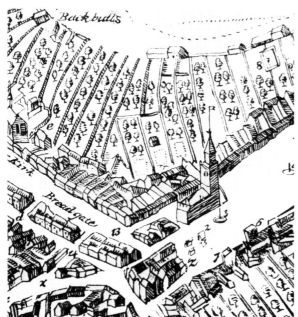

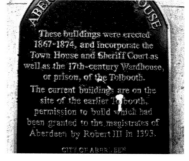

Above *The current sign outside the Tolbooth. (Photo by Geoff Holder)*

and locks, and low-vaulted windowless rooms, the interior resembles a set for a Gothic horror film, and conforms to what many people would regard as a classic 'haunted house'. On my visit, with only Chris Croly the curator, and my wife, for company, I found it grimly atmospheric, but despite spending ten to fifteen minutes alone in the darkened Jacobite Room, with its models of prisoners shackled to a metal bar in the stone floor, I did not pick up any sense of anything spooky.

In contrast, on a hot day in May 2007 author Graeme Milne was in the Crime and Punishment Room, on a tour with a group of eight people, when he felt icy cold down his left side; along with four others in his group he heard a sound like shuffling feet or a chain being moved close by. In his book *The Haunted North*, Milne also includes an episode related to him by a Mrs Wood. In 2005 she had seen the apparition of a man wearing a brown striped suit and a 1920s' trilby hat. His overall height was very small, as if he was cut off at the knees due to the floor level having been raised since his lifetime. The sighting was on the first floor of the Tolbooth. Unusually, the apparition noticed Mrs Wood, nodding its head at her, at which point she became very scared and left the museum.

Two of the massive doors that are still in place within the maze of prison cells and passages in the Tolbooth Museum. (Ségolène Dupuy)

Ghost-hunting in the twenty-first century

In recent years there has been an upsurge in small groups of like-minded individuals setting out to investigate locations that have the reputation of being haunted. Some of these groups have greater quality control than others when it comes to the rigour of collecting, reporting and interpreting data. The procedures of these groups vary, but typically there will be a mix of long-established tactics (use of mediums, lone and group vigils, and 'calling out' – asking any spirits present to make themselves known) and new technology (digital video cameras and audio recorders, digital thermometers to measure temperatures at a distance, and EMF meters to record any changes in the ambient electromagnetic frequencies; electrical devices, mains circuits and humans all have EMF fields, and it is assumed that ghosts can either affect EMF fields, or generate their own). Another typical procedure is the use of 'trigger objects', small items set up with a chalk outline around them; a video camera is often trained on the objects in an attempt to record any movement caused by invisible forces.

In general this tactical mix is thought to make the best of both subjective (internal, human-centred) experience and objective (external, technology-centred) recording. In practice, no matter how sophisticated the technology and competent the operators, most events recorded during a modern ghost-hunt tend to be subjective, subtle, even barely-noticeable, and inevitably require interpretation as to whether there is anything paranormal prowling about. Factors affecting this interpretation include: the belief systems of the participants; environmental sources (air-conditioning, central heating, draughts, infrasound, waterpipes, and noises from the external city); and the kind of group psychology that can develop on a ghost-hunt, where participants are typically in a heightened state of nervous arousal, and feelings of excitement, anxiety, paranoia, anticipation and 'paranormality' can easily be communicated and shared through the power of suggestion. Other factors may also be at work – as one Glasgow man in his twenties told this author, hanging out in darkened rooms at night in frightening circumstances is 'a great way to meet girls'. Victorian and Edwardian investigators used cutting-edge technology such as photography and film in their investigations, while the séance rooms of the period were often a hotbed of suppressed sexuality. In some respects then, modern ghost-hunts may have the gadget trappings of the twenty-first century, but are still repeating the paradigms of their nineteenth-century predecessors.

There is perhaps a high expectation that, with all the advantages of cool technical toys, contemporary ghost-hunts will deliver instant, dramatic results, the ideal experience for those seeking thrills, or irrefutable evidence for believers in survival after death. In practice, most properly-conducted paranormal investigations produce findings that are at best ambiguous, with suggestions that such-and-such a phenomenon *might* be of supernatural origin. Typical of this more cautious approach is the work of East of Scotland Paranormal (ESP). Since 2007 ESP has conducted several investigations in Aberdeen, some of which are discussed elsewhere in this book, while several are presented in this chapter.

ESP has conducted three investigations in the Tolbooth, on 11 December 2007, and 12 March and 20 August 2008. Recorded phenomena included fluctuations in temperature and humidity; a 'thick and muggy' atmosphere; odd noises such as something that sounded like the jangling of keys, footsteps, a loud 'breath' and a high-pitched whistle; a sense of presence or of being watched; possible human voices, including singing; feelings of despair or oppression;

and moving shadows such as a 'tall dark figure' and a man with a 'faded' appearance. The phenomena were not consistent across the several visits and did not appear to be concentrated on any particular cell – in fact, rooms that had been 'active' in one investigation produced nothing on subsequent visits.

The first investigation included several mediums, who reported a wide variety of impressions of people and events. Some of these were quite intriguing, such as one medium feeling the labour pains of a fifteen- or sixteen-year-old girl who died in childbirth in the prison, and the presence of young children (kidnapped children were indeed held in the building for a time – *see* The Green on page 30 for the full story). However, the investigation also demonstrated the potential weakness of relying on the subjective impressions of mediums. None of the impressions could be backed up by written records, and in one case the 'received information' was quite incorrect – a medium stated that the Civic Room had been used as some kind of place of worship, when in fact it was a late addition to the building and was built only to store civic documents.

Perhaps the most intriguing event took place on the third visit. In less than fifteen minutes, various members of the team heard or recorded a female voice in the Great Escapes Room, a large light 'anomaly' leaving the same room, then two successive loud bangs, one in the Jacobite Room and the other in the Civic Room.

ESP's detailed reports can be read on www.esparanormal.org.uk, where the team note that many of the phenomena could result from natural, physical or human causes (such as the age of the building, the seasonal differences between summer and winter, and sound pollution from the street or adjacent buildings such as the Court House, which may account for the jangling of keys). In addition, the brooding, slightly malevolent architecture, combined with even the slimmest knowledge of the Tolbooth's dark history, can create a sense of foreboding or anxiety in which mundane sights and sounds can be easily misinterpreted. ESP cautiously conclude, however, that some of what had been experienced *might* have been paranormal, although it is unclear if it is some kind of active, conscious entity, or an imprint, the non-conscious 'recording' of past events that are somehow being replayed.

The ghosts of Union Street

At 8.30 p.m. on a summer's evening in 1859, twenty-six-year-old Revd Spencer Nairne saw Miss Wallis, an acquaintance, strolling along Union Street. As they passed each other, Nairne turned round – but both Miss Wallis, and the man she was with, had vanished. In September Nairne met Miss Wallis again, this time in London, where she told him that she had had a similar experience – she and her brother had been on Union Street, spotted Nairne, and then looked round to find that he was nowhere to be seen. The strangest part of an already strange episode was that she had recorded the meeting in her journal, showing the event took place in July. But Nairne's diary, kept during his travels (he was about to leave Aberdeen on a holiday to Norway) had the encounter listed as 31 May. Somehow the pair had seen each other's double in the same place, but on different days in different months.

The account, penned by Nairne, appeared in *Lord Halifax's Ghost Book* in 1936. The book shows that this was not the first time Nairne had encountered a double. In 1850 or 1851, when

Two views of busy Union Street, site of the Reverend Nairne's meeting with an apparition. (Photos by Geoff Holder and Ségolène Dupuy)

he was seventeen, Nairne was sauntering slowly through the London suburb of Clapham, arm-in-arm with a schoolfellow named Henry Stone, when they passed their headmaster, Revd C. Pritchard, walking rapidly in the opposite direction. As custom required, both boys touched their hats, and although Pritchard didn't look at them he did return the salute. About two or three minutes later the reverend passed them again, even though it would have been impossible for him to run around another way. Nairne and Stone, although mind-boggled, did not ask Pritchard about it, and he never mentioned seeing them twice.

Norman Adams' book *Haunted Neuk* recounts an experience Michael Ross of Peterhead had when he was a child. As he and his mother passed the Mercat Cross in the Castlegate, he

The Mercat Cross on Castlegate, with the Salvation Army Citadel behind. (Ségolène Dupuy)

saw a strange woman, dressed in Victorian-era clothes, carrying a parasol and wearing small spectacles. She smiled at the boy, but when Ross said to his mother, 'That lady is smiling at me,' no such person was visible.

Rachael Hayward and Al Hayes of ESP also run ghost tours of Aberdeen centre. One evening they were waiting by the Mercat Cross, as the customers for the tour gathered, when they were approached by two community wardens who related the tale of the 'Mad Hatter', an apparition of a man apparently seen at the spot where he used to own a hat shop. According to the wardens the ghost was well-known, but neither Hayward nor Hayes had heard of it before, and knew nothing of the 'Mad Hatter'.

The Mad Hatter of Aberdeen was actually Samuel Martin, who ran a hat shop at 34 Union Street, on the corner with Broad Street, between 1842 and his death in 1888. His nickname perhaps over-exaggerates his eccentricity, which was merely that of a larger-than-life, flamboyant individual who was most famous for extravagant advertisements in the *Aberdeen Herald*. Over several decades, the self-styled 'People's Hatter' filled his publicity with patriotic and amusing opinions on politics, international affairs and war and peace, sometimes laced with eye-catching typographic jokes such as:

> ## SAMUEL MARTIN
> does not expect
> ## TO BE MADE A FIELD-MARSHALL

Other than the mention by the community wardens, and their assertion that the story is well-known, there appears to be no further record of sightings of the Mad Hatter. Also missing

Rachael Hayward and Al Hayes, of East of Scotland Paranormal, in their ghost tour costumes. (East of Scotland Paranormal)

A typical page of advertisements by Samuel Martin, the 'Mad Hatter of Aberdeen' who is supposed to haunt Union Street. (Author's Collection)

from the documentary record is the spirit that is alleged to grab the arms, ankles and throats of pedestrians on Union Street. The incidents are supposedly linked to the murder of a little girl, although it is not clear whether the spirit doing the grabbing is the murderer seeking new prey, or the victim trying to get help. Again, several people have told Hayes and Hayward that this story is 'well-known', but no-one has come forward with an actual encounter, so it may be a piece of urban folklore.

The Drummer Boy and the little girl of Correction Wynd

One of the occupational pleasures of running ghost tours is that people tell you ghost stories. Two more have come to light from customers or passers-by on the tours run by Rachael Hayward and Al Hayes. In both cases the stories were claimed to be 'well-known', although once again it has so far proved impossible to track down the details of an actual sighting (during the writing of this book I asked several people about these two stories: everyone had heard of them, but no-one could provide an actual source – they just seem to be stories that are passed around).

The first concerns the Drummer Boy of St Nicholas Lane. The lane runs from St Nicholas Street to Correction Wynd, parallel to Union Street, and is best identified by the feathers on the sign of the Prince of Wales pub. The back story is a tragic episode in Aberdeen's history. On 11 September 1644, during the period of the Civil Wars, the Marquis of Montrose wished to take the city for the King, Charles I. Montrose's forces were drawn up to the south-west of the city, opposed by a defending force of townsfolk led by Covenanters. Observing the standard customs of war, Montrose sent a herald and a drummer boy to negotiate surrender under a flag of truce. While the herald was in discussions – which resulted in the Covenanters rejecting the terms offered – the boy was given something to eat and tipped a piece of silver. However, on their way back to the Royalist lines, someone – it is not known who – fired a shot at the boy's back, killing him. Montrose, enraged at this atrocity under a flag of truce, unleashed his forces. The ensuing conflict, known as the Battle of Justice Mills, saw the defenders utterly overrun, 160 dying in the fighting. Even worse, Montrose, a general who usually displayed great judgement, allowed his army of Irish mercenaries to plunder, rape and murder their way through the town.

The fighting took place on the sloping ground between Justice Mill Lane, Bon-Accord Crescent, Hardgate and Union Glen. The negotiations had taken place in Alexander Findlater's house by The Green (south of what is now Union Street), while the Covenanter lines were between the Denburn valley and the Hardgate (further south-west). This meant that the drummer boy never set foot on the ground that is now St Nicholas Lane, never mind being killed there. There is no exact record of where he was shot, but judging by the descriptions of the battle and the geography of the day, it may have been somewhere around where Langstone Place, Bon-Accord Square or Bon-Accord Terrace are today – several hundred metres from St Nicholas Lane. I therefore suggest that 'the Drummer Boy of St Nicholas Lane' is an entirely spurious ghost, invented purely out of the pathos inherent in an innocent child being murdered during a time of war.

The second story is another widely-circulated tale, which may even be true. The convention goes that during the Second World War two soldiers were walking along Correction Wynd,

St Nicholas Lane, where a
ghostly drummer boy is said to
walk. (Photo by Geoff Holder)

The Marquis of Montrose, the victor
of the 1644 Battle of Justice Mills.
(Author's Collection)

Correction Wynd, where during
the Second World War a soldier
allegedly held the hand of a ghost
girl. (Photo by Geoff Holder)

the old cobbled street that runs past St Nicholas Kirk and under Union Street, when one found a little girl holding his hand. He pointed the tyke out to his companion – but the other soldier firmly stated that he could not see her. If it is relevant, Correction Wynd was the site of the medieval St Thomas's Hospital, built in the eighteenth century. Building works in 1902 uncovered bones from the hospital's burial ground.

Apparitions at the Arts Centre

The striking Neoclassical building of the Aberdeen Arts Centre at 31 King Street, with its front portico of Ionic columns and a two-storey tower based on the Tower of the Winds in Athens, was built in 1829-30 as the North Church, and converted to theatres and performance spaces in the 1950s. In July 2008, Nicky Cairney of Aberdeen Ghost Hunters investigated stories of hauntings at the centre, and posted the results on YouTube.

Verna, a volunteer at the arts centre, said in an interview that there had been several sightings of a woman nicknamed 'the housekeeper' in the top-floor flat above the centre itself (this space is now used for storage). The previous caretaker, Joe MacKay, along with his wife, had seen the apparition several times. A female guest from Wales got up in the night to visit the toilet, and in the corridor saw a lady with grey hair in a bun, wearing a white blouse and long grey skirt. The guest said 'hello' but the woman did not respond. The next day she asked about the other person staying in the flat, and when describing the woman was told she had seen 'the housekeeper'. On another occasion, a caretaker named David was locking up and turning off the lights in the Bridge, the part of the building linking the Children's Theatre to the Green Room, when he was shocked to see an 'illuminated face'.

Going down?

The vertical slab of St Nicholas House on Broad Street (soon to be demolished when Aberdeen Council moves its headquarters to Marischal College) was the site of a curious encounter in July 1998. As described in Dane Love's 2001 book *Scottish Spectres*, two female employees, strangers to each other, watched the figure of a man walk along a corridor and enter a lift. The doors closed for a few seconds, before opening again because one of the women had just pressed the button. Despite the fact that the lift had remained on the same floor as the women, it was now empty. The man had entered it scant seconds before – and had simply vanished. In some retellings of this sighting, it is reported that the phantom figure was female, not male.

Provost Skene's House

This splendid sixteenth-century building between Broad Street and Flourmill Lane started off as an upmarket townhouse for various nobles, being much changed and extended over the centuries. By the late 1800s, it and the area around it had decayed, and it became a lodging-house for the destitute and desperate. Fortunately, the structure survived the wholesale

The tower of the Aberdeen Arts Centre (formerly the North Church). (Ségolène Dupuy)

St Nicholas House on Broad Street in 2010. In 1998 two employees apparently saw a ghost take the lift. (Photo by Geoff Holder)

urban demolition of the twentieth century and is now an excellent museum, set out as a series of rooms fitted out in the style of various periods, with a great deal of furniture on long-term loan from London's Victoria and Albert Museum.

Author Graeme Milne has catalogued a number of spooky experiences in the building, including footsteps, a sense of presence, sensations of being pushed, and several sightings of a female apparition dressed in a bonnet and old-style dress. In 2009, during an investigation by the East of Scotland Paranormal group, a digital audio recorder picked up an anomalous sound that sounded like a human imitating an animal's growl. No-one was near the machine when the EVP (Electronic Voice Phenomena) was recorded and there was no other obvious source for this puzzling sound. EVP is the term used for the process where voices from a ghostly source are apparently picked up on audio recording equipment; it should be pointed out that these 'words' are rarely clear and often distorted, requiring a degree of interpretation (and possibly the ear of faith) to decipher them. Other examples of EVP were picked up in the staff-only attic room at the top of the building, while the team also reported moving shadows, the sound of breathing, a choking noise, unexplained electromagnetic frequency variations, light anomalies, and a chair moving (unfortunately this movement was not captured on camera).

As noted in the group's own report, many of the observed phenomena are probably natural in origin. As I found on my visit during a dreich December day, the old building is rife with echoes and noises carried through the confusing layout of rooms, corridors and staircases, and things rattle weirdly in the wind and rain, while city noises seep in from the streets around. On the other hand, the testimony for repeated sightings of the same apparition is impressive.

There is another strange story connected with the house, yet again an apparently folkloric story passed on to Rachael Hayward and Al Hayes by a customer on one of their ghost walks. The tale they were told was that in the dollhouse, within the room set up as a Victorian nursery, was a black-haired doll that had been donated to the collection because the owner was 'spooked' by it. The story went that she moved into an old house and discovered a collection of Victorian dolls in one of the rooms. Thereafter the doll in question kept being found in various different locations, when no-one had actually moved it. Eventually these episodes of apparently inexplicable relocation so unnerved the owner that she decided to donate the doll to Provost Skene's House.

The sixteenth-century Provost Skene's House, where several sightings of a female apparition have been recorded. (Photo by Geoff Holder)

Fictional ghost stories, horror films and folklore all recognise that some dolls can be creepy, so this tale intrigued me and I decided to follow it up. I contacted Alison Fraser, whose title is the Keeper (Applied Art) of Museums and Galleries at Aberdeen City Council, and the person responsible for the collection at Provost Skene's House. She kindly passed the request to the staff – some of whom have been at the museum for many years – and no-one had ever heard of this story. There are indeed two dark-haired dolls in the collection, one working a hand-held spindle, the other dressed in a striped skirt and hat. Both used to be in the introductory room, not the nursery, and are presently in storage. Nevertheless, neither these dolls, nor any of their other companions, have any strange stories associated with them. The haunted doll is, I'm afraid, make-believe.

Backstage ghosts at His Majesty's Theatre

Edi Swan's 2006 history of this Edwardian building, *His Majesty's Theatre: One Hundred Years of Glorious Damnation*, relates the tale of 'Jake the Ghost', apparently the spirit of sixty-nine-year-old John 'Jake' Murray, a stagehand killed by a stage hoist during a circus performance on 26 December 1942. The phenomena fell into several categories: audible (footsteps on the fly floor, and on Lambeth Walk, the long passage from the west balcony at the stage-left side of the building by St Mark's Church – the passage was once an entrance to the balcony but is now a fire escape); environmental (sudden drops in temperature on Lambeth Walk); a sense of presence (in 1980-2 Savage, the night-watchman's Alsatian, would sit with ears back and fur bristling at the top of the steps leading down from the balcony to Lambeth Walk, refusing to enter the corridor); and apparitional (stage manager Pete Thorpe saw a man in a brown dustcoat on the bridge behind the paint frame; the apparition disappeared before his eyes). Items would also be relocated – Swan's paintbrushes went missing, turning up several feet away.

Swan believed Jake had saved his life on two occasions, both times when he was working alone in the theatre. Once Swan broke an ankle and only managed to exit the closed building by crawling through a supposedly padlocked door to the street and hence to hospital, while at another time he blinded himself with paint and managed to get from the paint frame – the above-stage area where the backdrops are created on a huge wooden frame – to the prop room to wash his eyes, without falling into the several voids along the way. It has to be said that the first of these episodes does not provide strong evidence for supernatural intervention, as the door could have been accidentally left unlocked. The second case is more intriguing – the journey from the paint frame to the prop room involves negotiating an irregular route with several flights of stairs, both up and down, going through at least two doors, descending onto the stage, and avoiding both the orchestra pit and a large gaping hole in the stage used for bringing props up from the below-stage area. Doing all that when blinded is impressive, although it could be argued that Swan was on high mental alert, navigating a workspace he knew very well.

Significantly, when the old sail-like hemp backdrop flying system was replaced in 1980-2, many of the odd noises that had been heard over the years simply stopped. However, several staff at the theatre like the idea that Jake is keeping an eye on them, or at least is still present, and the ghost has been incorporated into the folklore of the building – in fact he seems to have

The statue of William Wallace points the way to His Majesty's Theatre. (Photo by Geoff Holder)

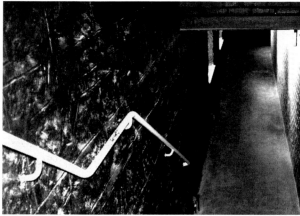

His Majesty's Theatre: 'Lambeth Walk', the fire escape from the west balcony. The watchman's guard dog refused to go down these steps. (Photo by Geoff Holder)

The paintframe above the stage. Here Edi Swan blinded himself with paint, and was allegedly guided downstairs to safety by Jake the Ghost. (Photo by Geoff Holder)

been adopted as the HMT's *genius loci*, its 'spirit of place'. Over the years everything that has gone missing, and any strange noises, have simply been blamed on Jake by default. So anything slightly unnerving – such as a heavy door slamming shut at the below-stage storage area – is jokingly put down to the ghost. And, I was told that a member of staff was working alone one day in what is now the corporate entertainment suite, but which used to be offices, when the cassette music player suddenly started playing at full blast. Of course, someone could have accidentally left the pause and play buttons depressed, and the pause eventually gave out, but it spooked the individual concerned. Theatres are associated with life, vitality, energy and crowds. When they are empty – and His Majesty's Theatre is no exception to this – the atmosphere changes and their echoing spaces and backstage labyrinths are almost inherently eerie. It seems possible that 'Jake' may have been the result of imagination playing on peculiar qualities of the building's own environment.

On the other hand – and, this being the realm of the paranormal, nothing is ever definitively one thing or another – after more than two decades of quiet, the phenomena may have returned during the major refurbishment in 2004-5. One Saturday afternoon, project manager David Steel was working in the theatre with the carpet layers when the sounds of someone walking in high heels were heard on the fly floor above the stage. A check showed that (a) the area was empty and (b) there was no-one wearing high heels in the building at the time. And, separate from 'Jake' (and the question of why he would be wearing female footwear), two performers saw the apparition of an old woman walking in the Stalls Bar (the bar to the right of the stalls as you look at the stage); she was identified as a long-serving barmaid named Miss Mitchell.

The unquiet library

Many authors have reported the phenomenon dubbed the 'library angel', some kind of subtle force that guides the researcher in a library to an unknown and unlooked-for book that actually turns out to be the perfect source for what they were searching for. Sometimes this guidance can be quite overt – the doyen of paranormal writers, Colin Wilson, has described how relevant volumes have fallen off his shelves at the right moment. The Central Library on Rosemount Viaduct was purpose-built as a library in 1892, the Children's Library being added in 1949. It is possible that the grand building has its own library angel in the form of George Milne Fraser, librarian here for fifty years, from 1889 to 1939. Fraser was also an author, his scholarly works including *Historical Aberdeen* (1904), *The Lone Shieling* (1908), *Aberdeen Street Names* (1911) and *The Old Deeside Road* (1921), all of which I have consulted when working on my previous books, *The Guide to Mysterious Aberdeenshire* and *The Guide to Mysterious Aberdeen*; much of those books, and this one, was researched in the Reference Library. If there is one ghost described in this volume that I would like to meet, it's G.M. Fraser.

However, the possible identification of the spirit as Mr Fraser comes from the single experience of a member of staff, who said the former chief librarian had helped her open a drawer at the desk in the Reference Library where he once worked. A second staff member reported the feeling of being watched after turning off the lights in the same location. The same man had a very unusual experience in the West Side Basement, when a ball of light passed right through his body, leaving him, in his own words, 'absolutely buzzing with energy'.

The Central Library. (Photo by Geoff Holder)

The West Side Basement in the library, where a member of staff encountered a mysterious ball of light. (East of Scotland Paranormal)

A third person from the library's staff claimed to feel uneasy in the West Side Basement, while CCTV cameras in the Children's Library had picked up some odd lights. All these reports were collected by the East of Scotland Paranormal Society (ESP) before undertaking two investigations, on 28 March and 4 June 2008.

The results from the two nights could not be more different. On the first visit, several of the team reported feeling uneasy in the West Side Basement, while the fully-charged camera battery drained (a commonly reported phenomenon on paranormal investigations). In the Children's Room various sounds were heard – knocks, footsteps, a scream or whistle, and what appeared to be a xylophone being played. This, however, was small beer compared to the team's experience in the Reference Library, where everyone reported a terrifying atmosphere and a genuine sense of fear. Curiously, the only actual phenomena reported were a minor camera malfunction and a woman's voice saying 'Hello'.

In contrast to the March investigation, when the Reference Library was revisited in June the atmosphere within was benign, and the only event of note was that some batteries drained quickly. Footsteps and a whisper were heard in the basement, while the faint sound of a bell was picked up in the Children's Room, and a chair may have moved (out of sight of the team) in the Conference Room. Various odd noises, including a whisper and a possible voice, were recorded on the mezzanine, although some of the sounds heard elsewhere were not audible on the recording equipment.

The ESP team noted that the March investigation took place on a chilly day, while the June one was conducted during high summer; it is possible, indeed likely, that temperature variations will cause a building of this age to contract slightly during the night, creating noises such as creaking and knocking. And, of course, the library is on a busy road in the city centre, with both residences and eating and drinking places nearby: sound pollution from these sources cannot be ruled out. Nevertheless, and despite the relatively subtle and low-level nature of the phenomena recorded, the team considered that there was definitely 'something' about the Central Library. Whether or not a long-serving, distinguished librarian still haunts the shelves, the cautious conclusion – as noted on their website – was that the building '*may* be experiencing phenomena of a paranormal nature'.

'Ah, there you are'

In the late 1950s, a young guard on night duty at the Old Customs House, 35 Regent Quay, noticed an icy presence in one room. Much more scarily, another night guard was alone in a ground-floor office at night when a voice said to him, 'Ah, there you are.' Things seem to have been quiet for a few years until 1974, when an officer, on his own in the building, was sitting in an easy chair when he saw a ghostly female figure bending over him. All of these experiences were recorded in Norman Adams' book *Haunted Neuk*. The three-storey Georgian building was erected by James Gordon of Cobairdy around 1771-2 as an elegant townhouse befitting a man of wealth and taste. Later it became a customs house and is now occupied by a number of organisations. I wrote to several of them, including the theatrical company Live Wire Productions; but, despite their interest in learning about their haunted heritage, none of the staff could report any encounters with the ethereal realm.

Market forces

The rather drab late 1960s façade of the Aberdeen New Market on Market Street (and its equally unattractive rear end on The Green) may not initially strike you as somewhere that is likely to be haunted, but appearances (and apparent age) can be deceptive. The site was originally part of The Green, the medieval thoroughfare and open-air market stance that was one of the ancient landmarks of the early city. In 1840-2, the celebrated Aberdeen architect Archibald Simpson created what many regarded as one of his masterpieces, a great covered market with a columned arcade and a second storey of shops overlooking the interior. It was rebuilt in a similar style after a fire in 1882, only to be obliterated by the extension of British Home Stores, resulting in the truncated and frankly ugly building of today.

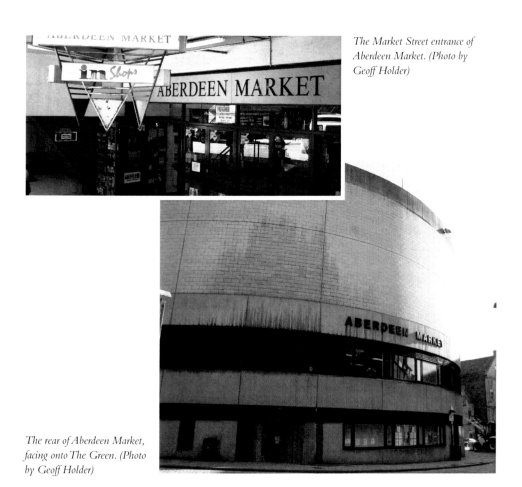

The Market Street entrance of Aberdeen Market. (Photo by Geoff Holder)

The rear of Aberdeen Market, facing onto The Green. (Photo by Geoff Holder)

John Dow, the manager of the Market Centre, told me that around 1995 a stall owner was closing up at the end of the day when, out of the corner of her eye, she saw a man in an old-fashioned coat walking past the shop. It was around 6 or 6.30 p.m. and the market should have been closed, so thinking that the man had sneaked in through an open door, the stall owner fetched a security guard. Both she and the guard checked all the doors, which were closed and locked, and searched the market – but no-one could be found. When questioned, the woman said the man was wearing clothes and a hat that were, in her own words, 'like Dick Turpin would wear' (the notorious English highwayman was executed in 1739; most illustrations show him wearing riding boots, knee-length britches, a three-quarter belted coat or a cloak, and a tricorn hat). This became a joke – people would ask, 'Has Dick Turpin been in today?' – but a while later a woman in her seventies came in, heard about the story, and said, 'It's not funny'. She had worked in the old market, possibly in the 1950s or '60s, and said the same figure had been seen several times.

John Dow also related how traders over the years had reported seeing a ghostly black cat. He had thought nothing of it until early one morning, around 2004, he came in early to open up and saw a black cat running up the steps from the food hall. He followed but could not see it again, and was puzzled that none of the motion sensors had been set off. He then stopped and thought, 'I've just seen the ghost cat!' It's possible, of course, that the cat was just a real moggie that knew its way around the market, and the motion sensors were simply not sensitive enough to pick up the crafty feline. Still, if the cat was a frequent visitor, the motion sensors should have gone off sometime …

Much more convincing was an episode 'a few years back' when John was working on the Union Street entrance of the market, pulling down an old ceiling. The area was always cold, and John often had a sense of being watched, and the hairs on the back of his neck rising up because he felt there was some kind of presence there. It was very dusty work and, when he returned to his office for a cup of tea, he was covered in stoor from head to foot. He wanted to ensure that no members of the public got into the working area while the ongoing alterations were underway, so had installed CCTV cameras. In the office, he and a security guard were watching the screen when, to their astonishment, they both saw footprints forming in the dust. The prints went up the very centre of the stairs before their eyes. 'Did you just see what I saw?' said one to the other. They rewound the tape, and in slow motion saw the faint outline of the front of a shoe where the footprints were being made. At this point in the interview I was agog – did he still have the tape? John had indeed kept the tape for months, fascinated by the footage – then one day someone accidentally erased it.

Another ghost was apparently caught on CCTV in the market during the summer of 2008. Robin Bradford, the no-nonsense security manager, told me how one morning he arrived via the back entrance, at 8 a.m. as usual, to see a man walking in the corridor between the market and Union Street. The door onto Union Street is always locked at night; if that were to be broken open, there was a second, much more solid, locked door at the entrance to the market one floor below. Between these two security doors there is a long, high-ceilinged corridor and two flights of stairs (this was the area where the flour footprints were seen). Seeing the man, Robin Bradford concluded that he was either a burglar or had somehow accidentally

Left *The corridor to the Union Street entrance where a ghostly figure was caught on CCTV cameras. (Photo by Geoff Holder)*

Below *The stairs from the Union Street corridor down to the inner market door. Footsteps were seen to appear in dust here. (Photo by Geoff Holder)*

been locked in all night, so he rushed out into the corridor – to find it was empty. Puzzled, Robin checked both inner and outer security doors – both were secure – and returned to the manager's office. But there, on the CCTV, was the man again, this time walking towards the (still-locked) door onto Union Street. The security camera there is situated above the door, pointing down the corridor; as the figure approached the camera, some distance before it reached the door, it simply vanished. Again, Robin sprinted up the stairs, once more to find the outside door locked and the corridor empty. There is no other exit.

Robin described the figure as wearing a big black hat, black clothes and a white shirt, which is partly consistent with the other sightings of apparitions in the market. He also thought the man was possibly black or Asian in appearance. In total, two CCTV cameras picked up the figure, the images being in black-and-white and taken every three seconds. Sadly the footage itself has not resurfaced.

John Dow wondered whether the phenomena had something to do with the tunnels stretching under the market. He had never been in them, and they were no longer accessible, but he recalled that his father had explored them a little, saying they were so dark he could not see his hand in front of his face.

Ghosts on The Green

Perhaps the most extraordinary haunting from this area is that which took place at No. 64 The Green from 2005 to 2008. During this period, the ground floor and basement were occupied by an exotic pet shop, Reptiles in The Green. I spoke to several staff and visitors during January 2010, and their reports were remarkably consistent. I have arranged their experiences by individual, with a little background detail on each person.

Witness 1: Diane Melville, thirty-something owner of Reptiles in The Green. Diane is a self-identified psychic with a deep interest in the supernatural. She owns a pair of large African sulcata tortoises, Stormin' Norman and Big Bertha, the chelonian couple being local celebrities.

Within the ground-floor shop, Diane witnessed the following phenomena. One of the most common incidents would be that the plastic boxes containing the live crickets and other insects would be found rearranged on the shelves at precise angles in perfect order. These boxes are around 12in high and long, by 6in wide. Bags of substrate for the animals, weighing up to 1kg, flew off the shelves (sometimes this happened in front of customers). Things would disappear, to be returned usually within an hour, although sometimes it took two weeks for them to reappear. Lights would flicker then switch on and off. The kettle switched itself on (a switch needs to be depressed to do this) and the tap would come on. The shop was lined with heated vivaria for the reptiles. One day there was the apparent sound of a large stone thrown into the gap between the vivaria and the wall, but there was no stone, and no-one to have thrown it. These events took place at all times of the day and night, and during all seasons of the year. There was also the frequent sound of childish giggling in the shop.

One evening Diane was working late, around 9.30 p.m., when she saw a man in front of the shop window. In Diane's words, he 'looked like Abraham Lincoln,' with a long black jacket and a bearded, thin face. He gave the sense of being 'out of place' or 'out of time' so she went outside to look for him, but he had gone. Could this be the same apparition seen in the Old King's Highway opposite? (*See* Chapter Five)

In contrast to the shop, which Diane thought had a happy, positive energy, the damp windowless basement or cellar gave off a sense of dark energy. The shop used the space for storage, but staff did not like to go down there on their own. Diane and others reported a feeling of being watched. Furthermore, the smoke detector went off ten times in a row, with no obvious reason.

Witness 2: Tom Lobban, a volunteer at the shop. Now sixteen years of age, he has worked at the shop at weekends and evenings since he was thirteen, and like the other staff I spoke to, loved exotic animals, being the owner of multiple snakes and other reptiles as well as numerous spiders and a scorpion. Before joining Reptiles in The Green he had no previous interest in the supernatural, and used to think ghosts were 'a load of rubbish'. 'It's a different story now!' he said.

Within the shop, Tom saw the wall clock – which was held up by a nail – come off the wall, but instead of dropping straight down it flew off into the middle of the floor. Once he took a lock off a 'viv' (vivarium) and put it down next to the tank while he performed his task. When he reached for the lock, it had been moved – and was found in a different part of the shop that he could not have reached absent-mindedly. Boxes and stacked goods on the shelves moved, 'Like someone behind the shelves was pushing them out.' Books stacked on top of the vivs were often pushed off into the 18in gap between the vivaria and the wall. Several times he heard a sound like a stone being thrown high off the tall vivs, although no missile was ever found. Heat bulbs in the vivaria would go off, and then switch on when the tank was unlocked and opened. This would be repeated, as if he was being played with. Lighting tubes flickered, lights would switch off, then on, then off again, and the phones would ring, but there was no-one at the other end of the line. Suspecting pranksters, the staff pressed call-back on 1471, to be told that the last call to the number was more than two hours before. The phenomena seemed to be more frequent in the evenings when the shop was quiet, and he thought that the incidents increased towards the time the business was due to move out of the premises – as if whatever it was did not want them to leave.

Tom did not hear the girlish giggling – but thought customers might have, as they sometimes asked if there were children in the shop. However, on several occasions he may have 'met' something. One evening, while having a cup of tea and sitting with his hands on his lap, he felt his hands being tapped with invisible fingers, as if each finger was exploring his hands. There was also the sensation of a hand being put into his. Then he could feel something gently poking his jacket – he saw the fabric being pressed, as if a hand was feeling and exploring the coat. Thereafter, the visits by the 'invisible fingers' occurred quite often, and they also used to play with Diane's hair.

Tom felt the shop had a happy atmosphere, but the basement was a different matter. Opening the door, he found that the lights he had switched off, sometimes just seconds before, were now on. The place gave him chills down his spine and caused the hairs on the back of his neck to stand up, so he tried to avoid going down there on his own. The smoke detector went off regularly, but the moment he went downstairs, the alarm ceased. Even if he responded within seconds, the ringing alarm would shut off as soon as he appeared. It was as if whatever was doing it was toying with him – but not in the playful manner associated with the vivs. Changing the batteries or the alarm made no difference to the phenomenon.

Witness 3: Bill Campbell, another volunteer at the shop, having been there since it opened. Another exotic animals buff, seventy-one-year-old Bill owns reptiles and birds of prey. He had no previous interest in the paranormal.

Bill heard the giggling, and sometimes the shop, although filled with heated vivaria, gave out a sensation 'like a fridge door opening'. One day he was sitting in the shop when he heard the sound of a stone whacking off the back of a viv. He rushed outside, thinking perhaps someone had thrown a stone through the window, but there was no damage, and no sign of a stone. The noise was repeated several times thereafter.

As for the basement, Bill too thought the smoke alarm was an act of mischief bordering on malevolence. It would ring, but switch off as soon as he reached the bottom of the stairs. Returning to the shop, the alarm would fire up again five minutes later, only to go silent the moment he went down.

Witness 4: Sean Jessiman, a friend of Diane. He occasionally did a bit of work at the shop, and his only experience there was that the basement felt very cold, and the hairs on the back of his neck stood up.

Witness 5: Francesca McDonald, a professional medium for forty years. She visited Reptiles in The Green to chat with her friend Diane, and they retreated to the basement to have a cup of tea and get out of the way of the busy shop. At this point Fran knew nothing about the phenomena. Whilst they were in the basement, Diane asked Fran if she picked up anything. Fran initially said no, then 'it was as if a veil dropped'. She perceived a horrifying scenario of children in rags, tied up and kept in bondage (her words were, 'Fear, desolation, abject misery.') The children were being held by a very unpleasant man giving off what she called 'a slaving energy'. He was tall and stocky, wearing a tricorn hat, and was angrily aware of Fran, screaming at her to get out. She also sensed there were tunnels somewhere nearby. Because she was not mentally prepared, as she normally was when working psychically, Fran suffered a headache and nausea for days afterwards.

Diane's recall of Fran's visit was that, in the shop, the medium additionally made contact with a girl aged between eight and ten, who said her name was Jennifer. She had a rag doll and was wearing a long white nightgown or smock, which looked 'poor but clean'. Jennifer did not like the 'zombies' in the basement – she said they were covered with lumps and were coughing blood, making Diane think of plague. Jennifer told the medium she did not like the music they were playing in the shop, said she was living somewhere dark and damp, and that her parents had gone to sleep and never woken up. Diane thought this meant they had been poisoned by gas leaking from the lamps, but another possibility is that the banked coal fire had consumed all of the oxygen in the room, and the pair had died of carbon monoxide poisoning – this was an unfortunately common form of death in the nineteenth century. The sense was that Jennifer was from a different period to the children imprisoned in the basement.

Witness 6: Tracy Gaitens, a professional medium who works under the name 'Gabriel'. She did a bit of volunteering at the shop, and while there Diane asked if she could sense anything.

Tracy was sitting behind the till when she saw something come off one of the shelves, as if it had been pushed. More things flew off the shelves when the shop was quiet, while ornaments and pictures would move. She had a sensation of her clothes being touched – the kind of tugging small children do when they want to attract your attention. She sensed the spirit was the wandering soul of a small child who did not want to leave, and enjoyed playing with things in the shop. She was a happy child, lively, rosy-cheeked, with blonde hair that needed a comb, and wearing a pinafore over her skirt.

The child in the shop was definitely from a later period than the poor wretches in the basement, whom Tracy also picked up on. The first time she went down into the cellar she was just doing Diane a favour, and had not been told anything about the previous experiences. But being in the basement on her own, she perceived a similar horror to that seen by Fran. There were boys, girls, young women, teenage boys and adult males, all neglected, filthy, abused, even starving, living on bread and water and struggling to keep warm in the dark and cold place. Many had not seen daylight for a long time, and some were gaunt and stick-thin, with infirm legs. They smelled of mothballs, body odour and decomposition.

These unfortunates were kept imprisoned by a burly, well-built man, whom Tracy perceived as a slave-master. He had a round stomach, unshaved full cheeks, a thin chin and piercing eyes giving out a frowning stare. He was in his fifties, wearing a flatcap and a waistcoat jacket over a top, and she thought he might have lived in the early 1800s. As with Fran, he was aware of Tracy, and screamed at her to get out.

What I found truly impressive about the visions in the basement was that Diane, Fran and Tracy all told me they knew nothing about the history of the area, and were puzzled by some of the things that had been picked up. All were genuinely surprised when I related the following.

During the eighteenth century, the British colonies in America were short of labour while British cities were overburdened with criminals, prostitutes, vagabonds, beggars, political agitators, religious non-conformists, the unemployed, the feckless, and the destitute. Conforming to the laws of supply and demand, the British authorities simply flushed out the jails and workhouses, and the colonies got the labour force they needed. The Aberdeen experience was slightly different, in that as well as adult undesirables, up to 600 'unwanted' children were unwillingly shipped off to the New World, where they were sold to colonists as 'indentured labour' for a specific amount of years, although 'slavery' was sometimes a more accurate term.

Although in theory the children were destitute or orphans, in practice any child who didn't look posh was kidnapped off the streets. The vicious trade was completely legal and above board, and made handsome profits for Aberdeen merchants and magistrates, middle-men, and ships' captains. Unfortunately for all these upstanding gentlemen, everything went awry when one victim, against all the odds, returned to Britain and denounced the deportation conspiracy for, in modern terms, what we would term 'violating his human rights'. In 1758, Peter Williamson, who had been kidnapped as a ten-year-old, came back and wrote a book attacking the Aberdeen magistrates. They responded in kind by prosecuting him, but he won a second case in Edinburgh and the Provost, the Dean of Guild and the four bailies of Aberdeen found themselves having to personally pay damages and costs to Williamson.

Because of Williamson's testimony and subsequent research, we know a little about the process involved in the kidnapping of children. They had to be imprisoned somewhere until

The current Reptiles in The Green shop, on Justice Street. (Photo by Geoff Holder)

sufficient numbers were gathered to be sold to a ship's captain as a job lot. Some children were incarcerated in the Tolbooth or in ships' holds – but others were kept somewhere on The Green. For at least two generations, Aberdonian children have been told about the sound of children screaming somewhere on The Green, sometimes accompanied by a phantom piper (the assumption is that the bagpipes camouflaged the cries of the forlorn). It would be truly extraordinary if further research revealed that the cellar of No. 64 had indeed been used as a holding place for kidnapped children.

In early 2010, after an extended refurbishment, the shop reopened as a tattoo parlour. The manager had spent some time converting the cellar (the site of many of the reported hauntings) and told me that not a single 'off' incident had been reported. Perhaps the phenomena have simply died out, or possibly they have relocated. In June 2008, Reptiles in The Green moved to a shop at Nos 1-3 Justice Street, by the Castlegate. Several people have reported odd things there. Diane Melville, Tom Lobban and Bill Campbell have all persistently smelled cigar smoke and floral perfume when there have been no customers in the shop, while Tracy Gaitens has picked up the cigar aroma and an unpleasant sickly smell, as if someone had just vomited. Tom has found that items stacked neatly in the storeroom have been disrupted, while Bill has heard thumping footsteps behind the vivaria, where no-one could be standing. There are also reports of shadows and cold spots, but it is certain that the phenomena are nowhere near as intense as that experienced when the shop was in The Green.

two

POLTERGEIST!

The ghost of Gordon Place

The most famous Aberdeen poltergeist was active in January 1920 at No. 1 Gordon Place, a now-demolished lane off Gordon Street, in the south-west part of the city centre. The building was one of a block of very modest – actually, miniscule – late-Victorian dwellings built for railway workers when the Joint Station terminal opened. The top floor of the two-storey building was occupied by the family of Alexander Urquhart, an ex-artillery man who now worked a laundry van. Husband, wife and four children were squeezed into a pair of tiny bedrooms and a cramped kitchen. On the night of 7 January, three of the children were asleep in one of the rooms, while the parents were sitting in front of the kitchen fire, with their invalid fourteen-year-old son, John, lying ill on a cot-bed in the corner. With the adults exhausted from work, money tight and distractions few, all was quiet.

Then – BANG! There was a great thump. The floor shook, the table and cot moved with the shock, and the dishes rattled in the cupboard. Tapping was heard from one wall, and then from the others. There was another almighty bang. Alexander, thinking perhaps it was some kind of explosion or structural collapse, sent a messenger to get the police. The first officer arrived just in time to catch the invalid teenager as another floor-shaking thump threw him out of his cot-bed. More policemen arrived, and proceeded to investigate the entire building, even clambering over the roof and chimney. Nothing was found, and after around nine hours of chaos in the darkness, the explosive noises and tappings ceased as the morning arrived. An officer was stationed at the house in case something else happened.

The sight of so much police activity within a narrow lane in a working-class district attracted an excited crowd. The police and municipal authorities considered various causes – trapped sewer gas, structural defects, subsidence, or the foundations being disturbed by a huge telephone pole planted at the side of house. But the crowd were having none of these dull, mundane suggestions. They knew what it was – the ghost of a former tenant in the basement of the disused smithy. The poor man was said to have committed suicide some years before.

Crowds and hauntings attract reporters, who know a good story when they see one. The 'ghost of Gordon Place' made it to the Aberdeen papers, and within a few hours it had flashed

The Urquhart family line up outside their 'haunted' house at 1 Gordon Place, from the Aberdeen Daily Journal *in 1920. (The Press & Journal)*

The Gordon Street area today; Gordon Place has completely vanished. (Photo by Geoff Holder)

around the news wires, and on 9 January people from Liverpool to London picked up their morning newspapers to read about the strange goings-on in a tiny close in Aberdeen. It was a sensation. Reporters were desperate for new angles, and were delighted when more noises were reported at night. The Urquharts were deluged with letters offering advice and instruction on dealing with the undead. An enterprising company from Derby circulated publicity for their 'psychic mascots', 144 of which cost 12s wholesale (around £18 in current terms, a real bargain when you consider they were 'guaranteed to give immunity from the dangers of the spirit world'). Then, as now, a visitation of the supernatural was often an opportunity for someone to make a quick buck.

It is worth noting that, at this stage, neither the authorities nor the Urquhart family thought there was anything paranormal about the incidents, and even some of the press suggested that the strange incidents had a perfectly ordinary cause – the London *Daily News* for 10 January noted, 'Aberdeen ghost laid low – prosaic explanation for strange sounds – nothing but a piece of wood that the wind had been knocking against a side of the house.' However, the notion of the 'haunted house' had gripped the provincial newspapers – not to mention the crowds who still hung around the lane. In this febrile atmosphere, with the tapping noises still ongoing, the spiritualists turned up. Spiritualism essentially is a belief system where the dead are thought to be communicating with the living, often by using raps or taps, or through the agency of a medium. Starting in America in the 1870s, it received a massive boost after the First World War and the influenza epidemic of 1918, both of which left millions grieving for their departed loved ones.

For the first séance held by the Bon Accord Spiritualist Association, thirteen people, including a female medium, the Urquhart family, and – very importantly – two reporters, squeezed into the confined house. No contact with the Other Side was made – the medium blaming the failure on 'unbelievers' within the sensation-hungry crowd milling around outside. A second séance was arranged, and this one was not merely successful – it was spectacular.

The séance took place at midnight (which suggests a degree of planning with an eye to the press – 'Midnight Séance' is a better headline than 'Séance at 10.37 p.m.'). Present were Mr and Mrs Urquhart, John and his brother, and eight other people, including the medium, who sat on the edge of the bed shared by the two boys. The presence of the children may suggest that the spiritualists suspected that one or other of the boys was the focus of the disturbance; then again, it may just be that the family members wanted to be there to see what all these important people were going to do in their overcrowded lodgings.

The gaslights were turned down and the medium went into a trance and contacted her usual spirit guide, an Irishman named Paddy. Paddy told her that the spirit of an old man was pacing the floor in an agitated manner. Alexander Urquhart 'recognised' the description as that of his deceased father. The medium then spoke in the voice of Urquhart Senior, calling out 'Alec!' three times and stating he had not completed a message he had intended to pass on at his deathbed. After something like sixty to ninety minutes, the medium was too exhausted to continue, and the lights were turned up.

At this point something truly odd happened. Fourteen-year-old John Urquhart sat up and said he could see his grandfather laughing at the foot of the bed, saying to him, 'Tell your faither to look after his mither.' John then became hysterical, stating he had been down in a 'black hole', and was scared in the dark, but then got out of the hole and saw the light in the room and his family around him. The spiritualists seized on this, telling the reporters: 'The manifestation proves the theory of Sir Arthur Conan Doyle, that the knockings are just the ringing of a psychic telephone bell, and that once the message is delivered, the summons of the spirit will cease.' Conan Doyle had lost his son in the war and had become an ardent spiritualist; his famous name was always being used by the movement as a form of 'celebrity endorsement', very useful when confronted with a sceptical public and a hostile Church.

According to one report, the Urquharts were so affected by the events at the séance that they became spiritualists, although this may have been speculation, or a temporary conversion caused by the crisis. Certainly the noises stopped, and were never heard again. John Urquhart survived into adulthood, bearing the unwelcome nickname 'Johnny Ghostie'. In the 1930s, the building was converted into the premises of a family of coach painters, J. Murray Smith. When reporter Bill Mackie of the *Evening Express* visited the firm in 1963, the Smiths told him that nothing strange had been seen or heard since they had moved in. Members of the family had even slept in the old kitchen and bedroom – the epicentres of the disturbances – while on fire-watching duty in the Second World War, and had experienced nothing. The building, however, retained its reputation with those who remembered the heady events of 1920. According to the Smiths, former local residents revisited the 'haunted' building from time to time, and in 1962 a retired police officer had popped in to reminisce about keeping an eye on the place during the 1920 flap. Sadly, Gordon Place and all the buildings on it have since been cleared away, and not a trace remains of what was once nicknamed 'Poltergeist Alley'.

It is hard not to get frustrated with the case of 'the ghost of Gordon Place'. It starts with strange noises and physical effects – classic poltergeist incidents – then, propelled by rumour, story-hungry reporters, and a spiritualist agenda, it proceeds from the restless ghost of a suicide, to communion with a deceased family member, and a sick child apparently having some kind of psychic episode. The initial thumps and taps remain unexplained, and I have some reservations as to whether they were actually connected to the incidents at the séance. Natural causes, group hysteria, hoax, media frenzy, peer pressure, psychological suggestion and a childish need to seek attention could all be factors, but we will never know whether there was anything genuinely paranormal about the events.

What is a poltergeist?

The word 'poltergeist' is of German origin, derived from the words *poltern* (meaning to make a loud noise, or to rumble or thud) and *geist* (ghost). It thus literally means 'noisy ghost'. The word was first used in print by Martin Luther (1483-1546), the instigator of the Protestant Reformation, but was introduced to the English-speaking public only in 1848, when Catherine Crowe's influential book, *The Night Side of Nature*, discussed several German cases. The term was popularised by the psychic investigator Harry Price, especially in a book from 1945 called *Poltergeist Over England*. Of course, long before the word was known, poltergeist-like incidents were being experienced, with recorded cases going back at least as far as the fourth century after Christ, while noisy, invisible spirits are known across all cultures. Poltergeists, it seems, are global.

Given that many 'polts' involve noises, the movement of objects, and annoying or destructive phenomena such as electrical interference, or fire-raising and influxes of water, all repeated over time, some parapsychologists prefer the phrase 'recurrent spontaneous psychokinesis' (RSPK). RSPK contains within its name an assumption that the poltergeist is a psychic human phenomenon (psychokinesis meaning 'moving objects by the mind'). Other researchers – especially those with a world-view inclined towards spiritualism or survival after death – regard the poltergeist as the ghost of a dead person, or some other actual entity or spirit. Both camps more-or-less agree that the poltergeist draws its energy from one of the humans present. In recent years, the orthodox thinking has been that the 'energy source' is a troubled child or adolescent within the household, but this cannot always be the case, as we shall see.

Parapsychologists and ghost-hunters love categories – partly because the process of assigning labels to things gives the illusion that order can be imposed on the chaotic world of paranormal phenomena – and in recent years a distinction has been drawn between 'poltergeist' activity (where the incidents seem to be focused on a person) and 'hauntings' (where the incidents are centred on the location). Poltergeist cases very rarely involve apparitions (visible ghosts). Of course, these are not clear-cut divisions, and it is perhaps more useful to think of paranormal phenomena as belonging to a spectrum of activity, where some cases are hauntings but with poltergeist-like features (such as the case at Reptiles in The Green – *see* Chapter One).

The Rosemount plate-thrower

If the attention of the newspapers may have been a factor in shaping how events proceeded at Gordon Place, the exact opposite took place in an apparent poltergeist outbreak in the Rosemount area of the city in the 1960s. A policeman answered a call to a disturbance at a house where a young person lived – to be met at the door by plates flying through the air, thrown by unseen forces. The investigating officer related his experience to a detective colleague, who passed the story on to journalist Norman Adams. Adams knew his source was reliable and trustworthy, but did not follow the story up, probably for reasons of confidentiality or sensitivity, and the story remained unreported until Adams briefly mentioned it in his 1998 book, *Haunted Scotland*. The detective concerned is now deceased, and whatever happened at Rosemount worked itself out without the glare of publicity.

A polt throws a tantrum

Norman Adams described two more minor poltergeist outbreaks. In the 1970s cushions, pens and other everyday objects were thrown around a room in a house in Osbourne Place. The owner got fed up with the daily outbreaks, and determined to remove the spirit. He discovered that a little girl had died in the house in the nineteenth century. So, the next time something moved through the air, he told the child off, using a 'disapproving parent' tone and mentioning the girl by name. The manifestations stopped. This does not, however, necessarily mean that the polt was really the ghost of the little girl – the literature of the paranormal is filled with cases where poltergeists seem to respond to names, sometimes several names at a time, depending on who is addressing them. It seems to be part of the 'game' polts play. You probably wouldn't believe everything a petty criminal said in real life, so why accept what you are told by a spirit that acts as the supernatural equivalent of a home-invading vandal?

The Fountainhall mystery

In 1875, Frederick George Lee, vicar of All Saints' Church in the London district of Lambeth, published a book entitled *Glimpses of the Supernatural*. As was often the case with Victorian works, the subtitle really tells us what it was about: *Being Facts, Records and Traditions Relating to Dreams, Omens, Miraculous Occurrences, Apparitions, Wraiths, Warnings, Second-Sight, Witchcraft, Necromancy, etc.* (I love the 'etc.'.)

The book included a curious poltergeist-like episode from Aberdeen. About 1865, an English clergyman took up the tenancy of 'an old-fashioned, pleasant-looking detached house, of some size and convenience … It had considerable grounds round it, well timbered, a high-walled garden, and was in many respects both commodious and comfortable.' It was also cheap. Soon after his family and servants moved in, however, strange things started to happen:

Noises of the most extraordinary character were heard in various parts. Sometimes there came the sound of heavy footsteps on the stairs. At other times there were knocks, both violent and gentle, at the doors, none of which could be accounted for. At midnight, on several occasions, there was a constant, uninterrupted sound in one room, as if a large sledgehammer (having been wrapped in a blanket folded several times) was steadily and regularly struck against the wall, at the head of the bed in the room, by some particularly powerful arms. 'Thump, thump, thump,' it sounded, as though lifted and directed with tremendous force; and this noise often lasted, with only slight intermission, for two or three hours. On other occasions, persons on the stairs or in the passages felt the air move, and heard the creaking of the floor close to them, as if someone invisible were passing quickly by.

On one occasion, everyone was awoken by a great crash, as if all the shutters had been forced open, so the clergyman took down a large presentation sword from the landing display and went in search of what he thought was burglars.

He first examined the dining room (from whence the noise seemed chiefly to come), but everything was just as usual. No shutter was open; no cupboards forced. So, too, in the hall and library. Nothing was moved. Then he descended into the large cellars; but there, likewise, everything was untouched, and nothing unusual was seen. A large retriever dog, however, which lay at the foot of the front stairs, was greatly agitated, and trembled and howled. But still nothing was to be seen, and perfect silence reigned. So the clergyman and his wife returned to their bedroom, only to hear, all of a sudden, precisely the same strange noise repeated about ten minutes after their return, with, if anything, even greater violence.

Even more extraordinary was an episode 'testified to by those who know the circumstances'. A young Scottish maid followed the sound of heavy footsteps up to an attic in the front of the house. Whatever she encountered there, she 'fell down in a swoon or fit at the top of the stairs; from that moment lost her reason, and is now in a lunatic asylum.' Seeking corroboration, Lee wrote to the clergyman's wife, who in June 1874 confirmed from her own personal knowledge that the account was 'neither understated nor exaggerated, but is in all its details strictly true and accurate'.

Up to this point the case consists of a number of unexplained and alarming noises, and an episode where a servant was badly affected by something, all reported by apparently reliable witnesses (Lee himself wrote: 'These are facts. As to the general accuracy of the foregoing, the Editor is enabled, on the testimony of several, to pledge his word thereto.') As with other cases, however, the seeking of an 'explanation' descended into the realm of rumour and speculation. It appears that the clergyman, or his wife, or someone else, made enquiries about the house's past. Several neighbours stated that the house had once belonged to a physician and university professor, who had received the property for free on the condition that he married the cast-off mistress of a Scottish aristocrat, the man who actually owned the land. The avaricious academic acceded to the bargain, but regarded the woman as a burden. So, after a short time, he murdered his wife and buried her body on the premises.

Such was the rumour, one that has been frequently repeated over the years. But the reality is very different. The place where all this took place was called Fountainhall House, now on Blenheim Place, in the West End of the city. It was indeed the home of a university professor. But he did not receive the property for free, did not murder his wife (she outlived him by a number of years), and the malicious rumour about him is deeply puzzling.

Dr Patrick Copland was Professor of Mathematics and Natural Philosophy – the former term for physics – at Marischal College for forty-seven years, from 1775 to 1822. Born in 1748 in relatively humble circumstances (he was the son of a country minister), he went on to become one of the leading scientific figures in pre-Victorian Aberdeen, not only inspiring generations of students but also popularising scientific subjects with lectures and demonstrations for working men's self-improvement societies and other extramural adult education classes. He was consulted on matters as varied as the hydraulics involved in ensuring a reliable and pure water-supply for Aberdeen, accurate weights and measures for the city, surveying, industrial bleaching, and much else. He was an intensely practical man, building his own lathes and tools, and deeply involved in the engineering issues of his day. When Dr John S. Reid wrote a sketch of Copland's life for the *Aberdeen University Review* in 1985, he went through the family papers and related correspondence, and could find no derogatory comments on his character: he seems to have been universally admired.

The rumour about his marrying 'the cast-off mistress of a Scottish aristocrat' probably derived from a distorted and confused view of some known aspects of Copland's life. Firstly, he became a firm friend of Alexander, 4th Duke of Gordon, an intellectual interested in astronomy, mechanics, developing his vast estate and improving the lot of his tenants. The two collaborated on many projects, and from the surviving correspondence it is clear that the duke treated Copland as an equal, despite the class chasm between them. In 1787, Copland and the duke visited Switzerland and eleven years later they both paid court to master-inventor James Watt in Birmingham. Gordon introduced Copland to a different echelon of society, and many of Copland's later commissions from aristocrats sprang from this. The duke was also Chancellor of King's College, which would have done Copland's academic career no harm.

In addition, the young Copland was popular with the ladies. Tall, handsome and strikingly dressed, he was always welcome at Aberdeen's social balls, and no doubt many an aristocratic ingénue must have fluttered her fan when his commanding presence hove into view. But Copland did not marry until he was thirty-nine, his bride being Elizabeth Ogilvie, almost twenty years younger; she was the daughter of a surgeon in the Royal Navy. They had four children.

For something like fifteen years, the professor and his family lived in college lodgings. Then, in 1803, they moved into Fountainhall House. It was certainly not a 'gift': the house had been built by merchant Alexander Dyce in 1753 or so, and Copland purchased it from the estate of George Skene, his predecessor in the chair of natural philosophy. Perhaps the idea that it had been 'free' came from a much earlier episode: when Patrick Copland and Elizabeth Ogilvie were married, the Duke of Gordon offered them Glenfiddich Lodge for their honeymoon.

In 1803, when he occupied Fountainhall, Copland was fifty-five years old. He was distinguished, fêted, and finally earning a respectable income. To his neighbours he may have been a slightly intriguing figure, a middle-aged academic perhaps with the minor eccentricities that often go with the role. But why anyone would have thought he had murdered his wife – when both Elizabeth and the four children were much in evidence – is a mystery, although it may have something to do with the fact that in his later years Copland's family appear to have moved back to college lodgings, possibly because he was ill. Copland himself died at Fountainhall in 1822, probably of throat cancer.

As for the anonymous clergyman of the report in Lee's book, after some digging in Church records, I think this may have been Revd Robert Skinner, incumbent from 1856-69 at St Andrew's Episcopal Church (now St Andrew's Cathedral) on King Street. Lee describes him as English: Skinner was from Durham. His wife was Annie Henrietta, *née* Sangster.

As we have seen, the whole 'murdered woman under the floorboards' rumour had no substance. In my opinion, this derailed the initial report, which is fascinating enough in itself. Just what caused those loud, dreadful bangs and crashes? What happened to the maid? Unfortunately nothing more was written on the subject, and another of Aberdeen's 'noisy ghosts' will remain a mystery forever.

three

THERE'S A GHOST IN MY HOUSE

Houses have distinct personalities, either bequeathed to them by their builders or tenants, absorbed from their materials, or emanating from the general environment.

William Beebe, *Edge of the Jungle*, 1921

It may be surprising to learn that the places which are often thought of as being 'spooky' – graveyards, ruined buildings and so on – actually produce very few accounts of ghosts. In fact, the most common place where people see apparitions is in the home. (Apparitions are visible figures; however, in many hauntings the spirit does not reveal itself visually.)

The shrouded spirit

In the middle of the night in 1958, an elderly widow woke up in the upstairs bedroom of her 200-year-old house in Froghall Terrace. Moving slowly from the direction of the room's tiny window was a figure garbed in a white shroud. The widow's twenty-two-year-old daughter, a bus conductor, was sleeping in the same room. She also woke up and saw the ghost. As the apparition moved towards them, both women screamed and the figure disappeared. Thereafter, both mother and daughter slept downstairs out of fear, but the ghost was not storey-specific: at a later date it appeared, standing by the piano, to a young female guest who was sleeping in a downstairs room. Screaming, she leapt out of bed, ran into the neighbouring room, and jumped in with the other two women. No further descriptions were forthcoming, the incidents being reported in the *Press & Journal* on 4 April. The widow was interviewed and stated her belief that the ghost was a death omen, the rather shaky rationalisation being that the bedroom window overlooked the cottage where her brother-in-law had been born; at the time of the first manifestation he had been very ill, and died a few weeks later.

The semi-naked servant

In 1935, eighteen-year-old James Mann arrived at his substantial family home, some twelve miles from Aberdeen, to find the entire house unexpectedly full of relatives who had recently returned from India. As a result he had to sleep in a small bedroom on the ground floor. There was no electric light so he settled down to read his favourite book by the light of an oil lamp. Sometime after midnight, he looked up to see a girl in her twenties materialising through the wall. She had jet-black hair drawn tightly in a bun and was wearing a petticoat. She also had a sense of transparency about her, and was naked to the waist. 'What are you doing here?' asked the teenager, no doubt surprised to find a semi-nude spirit in his room; in response the girl merely smiled slightly, then vanished. The whole encounter had lasted less than two minutes. Later, Mann compared notes with a relative who had witnessed the same apparition, possibly on the same date during a previous year. The family rumour was that an old recluse once lived in the house, his only companion being a young maidservant. She apparently disappeared in mysterious circumstances, and her body was never found. Such was the speculation, but Mann could find nothing more. The experience had a profound impact on him, and by the time he was interviewed by the *Evening Express* on 14 January 1969, the fifty-two-year-old chartered accountant had been hunting ghosts for decades.

The silent monks

Norman Adams collected two tales of ghostly monks. In the early 1960s a nurse from Edinburgh, staying at genteel lodgings in the West End, saw a silent, faceless, monk-like figure at the foot of her bed at least twelve times over a five-week period. And sometime in the early part of the century, a young lass from the country, staying in lodgings in Wales Street in the eastern part of the city, saw almost exactly the same thing – a silent, faceless monk (the first tale is from Adams' *Haunted Scotland*, while the second is in his earlier book, *Haunted Neuk*). The two sightings, separated by geography and several decades, are remarkably similar – not just in form, but in the fact that each was seen by a young woman staying in strange surroundings, each was faceless and silent, and neither location was ever occupied by a monastery or any religious institution.

Partial ghosts

Sometimes the form of the ghost seems to have undergone some kind of drastic supernatural surgery. The apparition of an old woman seen in Devanha House, in the Ferryhill district, was distinguished by her white nightgown, straggly grey hair – and the complete absence of any form below the waist. The mansion was built in 1813 for William Black, owner of the nearby Devanha Brewery on the riverside ('Devana' was the name the Romano-Greek geographer Ptolemy gave to the area in his *Geographia* of AD 146). In 1840, the rather plain house was given a major facelift, with curved wings added at each end, and major internal remodelling. The venerable lady may have been a phantom of the original house, her favourite haunts (and her legs) truncated by the alterations in the levels of the floors. She was apparently still being glimpsed in the 1990s by the employees of the company that then occupied the mansion, but since the building's conversion to flats she appears to have moved out.

Another bizarrely configured spirit was seen by young Neil Mackenzie in his family's fourth-floor flat in Great Western Road. He woke up to see a man sitting on a horse in the old-fashioned mirror in his bedroom. Yet the image was not just *in* the mirror – the front half of the horse was in the room itself, its hooves vanishing below the floorboards, while the front and end of the rider's long lance disappeared in the ceiling and floor respectively. (This is another incident from *Haunted Neuk*.)

The sleep of reason brings forth monsters

You will have noticed that many of the aforementioned reports involve witnesses waking up from sleep. This may be very significant, because strange things happen to the human brain at the edge of sleep. In some cases our minds, rising from sleep, may be semi-alert and vaguely aware of the surrounding environment, but the body has not yet woken up. This can give rise to feelings of 'sleep paralysis', or a sense that some malevolent entity (such as a spirit, demon or alien) has you in its power, unable to move. A related situation is where our muscles twitch in our sleep without our control (known as hypnic jerks), a state where we can imagine we are moving, being attacked, and so on.

In addition, as the brain makes the transition from sleep to the wakened state, we are briefly in a 'no-man's land' (or, more accurately, a 'no-mind's land') where we are susceptible to auditory and visual hallucinations, known as hypnagogic hallucinations or hypnagogic dreaming. Anyone can experience this hypnagogia (also known as phantasmata), and probably everyone has done so at least several times in their lifetime. Usually we just shake the strange sensations off in the process of waking up, but sometimes our drowsy brains don't catch up in time and powerful, 'real feel' temporary hallucinations can be experienced. This hypnagogic imagery can sometimes be interpreted as ghosts. This is not to say that all of the cases above involve hypnagogic hallucinations, but some certainly might. It's something to bear in mind when examining cases where people have woken up to find a ghost in their bedroom.

Invisible visitors

Sometimes domestic ghosts do not show themselves to the eye, apparently determining to pique our other senses. On 20 September 1979, the *Evening Express* carried an interview with William and Moyra Russell, the long-term live-in guardians of the Church of Scotland's Deeford hostel at 59 Riverside Drive. Deeford was home for disadvantaged boys doing apprenticeships in Aberdeen. For nearly twenty years the Russells had been visited by an invisible ghost they called Mary. Lights would go on and off, and there were the sounds of a girl's skirts swishing, or noises of glass breaking – although no damage was ever found. The Russells believed Mary had been the daughter of an Aberdeen minister. When her illegitimate child was taken away from her she committed suicide in a second-floor bedroom. Because of her loss, she was always

The former Deeford hostel on Riverside Drive, now private dwellings. (Photo by Geoff Holder)

The novelist Alanna Knight. (Alanna Knight)

happy and active when children were in the building. However, some six years previously the inside of the house was altered for fire regulations, with internal walls knocked down and passageways opened up. Since the remodelling nothing had been heard of Mary – 'I think she's got lost,' said Mr Russell. The couple were moving out because the hostel was closing, and were wondering what would become of their favourite ghost – 'Perhaps she'll come and live with us – she's always been very good to us,' said Mrs Russell. From 1980 to 2003, the nineteenth-century B-listed building was a centre for the treatment of addiction, and after a brief period as a care home it has been extended and turned into flats. There have been no further reports of Mary.

In the 1950s, when novelist Alanna Knight was recently married, she and her husband Alistair were tenants in a house on Springbank Terrace, on the edge of Ferryhill. The rest of the building was empty, and Knight had to cook meals in the basement kitchen and carry them up to their flat on the second floor. She hated the basement, not merely because its stone-flagged floor was cold and reeked of damp, but because she always felt someone was standing behind her when she was at the cooker or sink. This sense of presence was so strong that on evenings when her husband was out tutoring she avoided going into the kitchen altogether, although she did not mention her fears to him. To add to the slightly unnerving atmosphere, heavy doors would bang on windless days. On one occasion – as she remembered in an article in the *Evening Express* on 2 November 1968 – she was collecting the milk from the doorstep on Sunday morning when the front door slammed shut, leaving her with nothing but a transparent nightie to protect her from the disapproving glares of people on their way to church. Of course, all of these incidents do not stack up into strong evidence for ghostly activity, but when the couple moved into a new house a short while later, Alistair said: 'I'm not sorry to be leaving. Funny place, that kitchen. I always feel as if someone's creeping up on me. I used to think it was you, but when I turned round, there wasn't anyone there. I don't suppose you've noticed?'

For a few months during the First World War, Kath Innes lived in the attic rooms at No. 27 Blackfriars Street with her mother while Kath's father was fighting with the Gordon

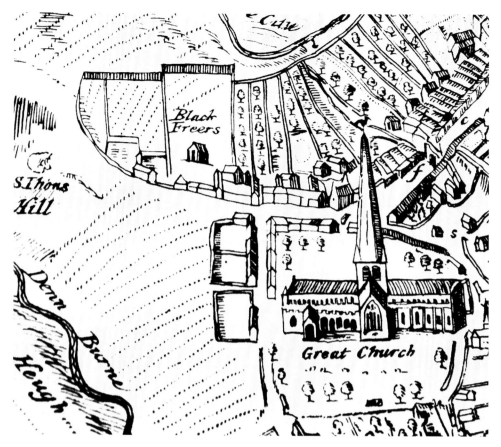

A seventeenth-century view showing the site of the destroyed Dominican Friary ('Black Freers'), later the allegedly haunted Blackfriars Street. (Author's Collection)

Highlanders on the Western Front. Along with its neighbours, the house was erected in the early nineteenth century on the site of the Dominican Friary, founded by the Black Friars in the thirteenth century and destroyed at the Reformation in 1559; a number of skeletons from the friary graveyard were found nearby during various building works. After they moved in, Kath and her mother learned the place was 'no' canny'. A neighbour was wakened by the sound of bare feet on the kitchen floor, and the footsteps stopped at the mantelpiece. The woman checked the other members of the family, all of whom were asleep. Next morning she received a message that her son had been killed in France. Kath and her mother were chatting with another elderly neighbour at the woman's door when a loud crash was heard from within. The old woman went into the empty house to find the heavy family Bible had fallen from the top of the chest of drawers in her bedroom, and landed flat on the floor. Another time, Kath's mother was telling her off after a domestic accident when a loud knocking came at the door. 'We both got a shock and when my mother opened the door there was nobody there! The house had a bare wooden floor yet not a footstep was heard going up or down.' Kath shared her memories in *Leopard* magazine in January 1990, by then aged eighty-two. No. 27 has now been demolished and the site is part of the complex surrounding Robert Gordon's University.

The evil dead

By and large, if some of the ghosts already described have not been entirely benevolent, at least they have not been outright malevolent. But some spirits are not such genial companions. Some, in fact, seem positively murderous.

Take the case of Diane Samat. In this case the background is important. Diane had three children from a previous marriage, and in 1976 married her new husband, Isa, a Malaysian studying dietetics at Aberdeen. They set up home in Garthdee. In July 1976 she woke up at 2 a.m. to a sensation of dreadful cold and an inexplicable panic. As Isa continued to sleep peacefully next to her, Diane saw the apparition of a tall, gaunt, brown-skinned woman with untidy grey hair standing at the bedroom door. Despite the room being pitch black, the figure appeared to be lit internally, as if there was a candle inside her. She was wearing a yellow and grey dress patterned with a kind of diamond check design, with the sleeves rolled up.

Diane shook her head, and closed and opened her eyes in an attempt to make sure she was awake and not dreaming. But instead of vanishing like a figment of sleep, the old woman advanced on Diane and closed talon-like hands around her throat. Diane struggled to free the grip of the corpse-cold fingers, but the intensity of the attack grew and she knew she was going to be strangled to death. Despite the struggle, her husband continued to sleep soundly. Then, for no reason, the ghostly assailant simply walked away with a sneer, leaving behind the distinct impression that she was telepathically communicating the message, 'And now you'll believe in ghosts, and now you'll believe in ghosts.' As Diane screamed, the apparition moved as if to leave via the door but then suddenly faded away. The screaming woke Isa, who was confronted with his incoherent wife clutching her neck and chest, both of which were sore for days afterwards.

Thinking about the experience, Diane wondered if the apparition had been the flat's previous occupant, a widow who had lived there for forty years and died there. But Isa reacted strongly to her description of the ghost, eventually revealing that it matched that of his grandmother, who had raised him in Molucca until she had died when he was six years old (the only thing that did not quite match was the yellow and grey diamond-patterned dress – Grandmother Samat always wore a garment of the same colours, but in a floral pattern). She had been a domineering, jealous and possessive woman who interfered in every aspect of her husband's life – in fact the man, who was still living in Malaysia, continued to feel her presence, sensing that she was still prying into his affairs, and entering his dreams. Presumably she had an animus against her grandson's new wife – or perhaps the visit was simply a warning for Diane to look after her husband *or else* – and for the next few weeks Diane slept with the light on, although there were no more attacks. Diane Samat recounted her frightening experience in Peter Moss' book of first-person paranormal accounts, *Ghosts over Britain*, the details later being expanded in *Is Anybody There?*, a book of supernatural investigations by Church of Scotland minister Stewart Lamont.

Also in Garthdee, Moira Robertson woke up to find herself floating about 2ft above the bed, menaced by dark shapes, whispering voices, and buzzing noises. Distorted words came from her throat, like a slowed-down tape player, although she was unable to shout to her partner, whom she could hear in the bathroom. Suddenly she was back on the bed and everything was normal. This 1998 episode was collected by author Ron Halliday in his book *Evil Scotland*. The same work catalogued the case of Jennifer Morgan. In the 1990s, Jennifer moved into a semi-detached council house in a village just outside Aberdeen. After living there for around two weeks she was regularly attacked in her bedroom, invisible hands closing round her throat as she slept. She had the impression that the assailant wanted to take over her body. The attacks only ceased when Jennifer moved out of the house.

Even more alarming is a case from a converted nineteenth-century gatehouse on the outskirts of Aberdeen. When a couple in their twenties, with a small child, moved in, there was nothing strange about the place. But after a time they heard persistent noises like footsteps, both upstairs and on the stairs. Eventually, the terrified family moved out for one night to allow psychic Tom Rannachan to conduct an after-dark vigil. Over the next few hours he encountered a whole range of phenomena. There were noises (footsteps on the staircase, crashes, thumps, doors slamming shut upstairs, sounds of dragging, heavy breathing, smashing glass, and a male voice calling 'Thomas'); putrid smells like vomit and severe body odour came and went; and the electrics went haywire: the television came on at full volume, the lights fused several times, forcing Tom to operate by torchlight – and then, when the new torch battery drained, by candlelight. Physical phenomena included the handle of the toilet door turning while Tom watched, and the handle of the kitchen door rattling. At some point Tom found four deep scratches on his neck, but had no idea how he got them.

As Tom admitted in his book *Psychic Scotland*, he was terrified, and had the distinct sense he was being toyed with by a presence that was undeniably evil. Two apparitions manifested at several times, and both interacted with him. One was a woman in dark clothes and her hair in a bun. She had piercing eyes, and when Tom questioned her she screamed at him and vanished. Tom got the impression that she was the victim or spirit-slave of the real source of the pandemonium – a man 6ft 6in (1.98m) tall, with long hair, a balding crown and straggly sideburns. Tom saw and smelt him several times, and felt the man was hunting him, rampaging through the property, banging on doors and shouting his name. Tom ran from room to room to escape, but eventually faced his persecutor, praying out loud and shouting at him to leave. After about thirty minutes, the house became quiet and there were no more disturbances that night.

Of course there is no independent corroboration of this most extraordinary of episodes, but apparently the family moved back in and their lives remained spook-free, so perhaps the two unquiet spirits had indeed been banished.

Crisis visitations

This is the term given to the spirit of a living person that appears at a distant location near the time of death. Typically, the spirit visits a friend or loved one, often as a visible apparition. A good example is in Catherine Crowe's pioneering study *The Night Side of Nature*. Mrs K. was sitting in the parlour of her husband's manse in Aberdeen when she saw her brother pass the window and look in. The couple went to the front door to greet their visitor, but no sign of him could be seen. Checks at the back door and with the servants turned up nothing. The woman was convinced that she had seen her brother, and later news was received that, around the time of the incident, he had died suddenly at his home. Crowe had picked up the story from one of Mrs K.'s relatives, and had had it confirmed by a close friend of the family. The interest here is that Crowe describes Mrs K. as the sister of Provost B. of Aberdeen.

Crowe's book was published in 1848, so 'Provost B.' must have been either Alexander Brown (Provost 1826-8), or James Ogilvie Blaikie (Provost 1833-6, died 3 October 1836).

A similar, but more dramatic, account can be found in the *Journal of the Society for Psychical Research* for October 1885. In 1883, Mrs Elizabeth Duthie of Edinburgh had been worried about the health of her close friend Miss Grant of Aberdeen. On 23 August, Mrs Duthie retired to bed at 8 p.m. An hour later, she was lying half asleep when she felt that someone was bending over her. She opened her eyes to see the face of her friend, Miss Grant. Seconds later the figure left the room, and a search of the premises found no-one present. The following evening, Mrs Duthie received the news that Miss Grant had passed away around 9 p.m. in Aberdeen, the same time her friend had seen her in Edinburgh.

When he was a teenager, James Mann was told that a relative's father had died when his son was still quite young. This obviously meant that when the young man later got married, his father was not around. For some reason, however, the bride's mother expressed a strong desire to meet the deceased gentleman, a wish she repeated many times over a long life. When the lady became ill in her old age, her daughter went to live with her while the daughter's husband, Mann's relative, stayed at home. One night the man had just got into bed when the apparition of his mother-in-law entered. She looked very pleased and told her son-in-law: 'I'm so happy; I've just met your father.' As the spirit vanished, the phone rang. The caller bore news that the old woman had just passed away, in her daughter's arms, some fifty miles away. Mann's story appeared in the *Evening Express* on 14 January 1969.

Another crisis apparition was reported in the *Dundee Courier* in December 1904. An old woman from Portlethen, huddling round her fire one cold December night, saw a pale face pressed against the window pane. She recognised it as her daughter, who had emigrated to Canada, and rushed to the door – but the spectre had vanished. A week later the woman received a letter from overseas stating that her daughter had died – at the exact date and time that the pale face had appeared at the window.

Sometimes the visitation is less direct. *Phantasms of the Living*, published by the Society for Psychical Research, contains a letter from Mr S.N. Wilkinson, J.P., from Stockport. In March 1881 he had been staying in Blackpool, and around teatime 'felt a strong conviction of some unknown evil which made me perfectly restless.' The sensation was 'quite unique in its strength, preventing him from settling to anything.' Two days later Wilkinson arrived home to find a telegram from Aberdeen, stating that one of his closest friends had died on the day he had had the presentiment.

Death warning in the corn

Many noble Scottish families have a legend that there will be some kind of supernatural indication that a prominent family member is about to die, or disaster is about to strike. Most of these omens take the form of strange cries or noises, or apparitions of humans or spectral animals, or visits by certain species of bird or beast. Culter House, north of Peterculter, has (or had) what is – as far as I know – the only paranormal portent that is agricultural in nature.

The grand mansion was built in the 1670s by the flamboyant, extravagant Cumins of Culter, on the site of an older medieval predecessor. Above the main door was placed the Cumin

A garb or sheaf of corn, the heraldic device of the Cumins of Culter. The appearance of the garb presages disaster. (Author's Collection)

coat of arms – a pair of ostriches bearing the Cumin crest, accompanied by three garbs (an old-fashioned word meaning sheaves of corn). And whenever disaster is on its way, a falling sheaf of corn is seen. Intriguingly, the portent seems to have stayed loyal to the house, rather than the family. In 1729, the Cumins vacated the property, to be replaced by the Duffs, who in turn sold it in 1908 to Theodore Crombie, a member of the wealthy industrialist family who ran Grandholm Mills on the River Don. Two years later, a falling sheaf of corn was seen, and fire broke out, probably as the result of the carelessness of a workman undertaking Crombie's alterations. The King James Room and Ballroom were gutted, but Crombie restored and extended the mansion, which has since gone through a number of owners and uses, including four decades as the Boarding House of St Margaret's School for Girls. The sheaf of corn has not been seen since the fire of 1910.

Investigations in private homes

In November 2007, East of Scotland Paranormal (ESP) conducted an investigation in a flat on Marischal Street. The houses here were mostly built in the late eighteenth century, when the street was laid out from the high ground of Castlegate down to the docks, spanning Virginia Street and thus becoming Aberdeen's first flyover. There had been previous reports from the flat from female tenants, who felt the frightening presence of someone looking into the lounge from the hallway, as well as sounds of scratching and dragging, light bulbs frequently blowing, and the front door regularly opening on its own – even after having been firmly shut again. Other logged phenomena included cold spots, and flashes of movement seen out of the corner of the eye. Obviously it is not hard to find prosaic explanations for most – if not all – of these events, but clearly the residents were anxious about living there.

Perhaps inevitably, the investigation recorded various phenomenological bric-a-brac that could possibly have been paranormal. On one occasion, there was a very sharp, very rapid temperature drop, while at other times some investigators complained of feeling hot and uncomfortable. Moving shadows, flashes and apparent variations in light intensity were glimpsed, and several people felt as if they had been lightly touched. The medium on the team picked up the spirit presence which seems to look into the lounge; it was a former butler, apparently named Edward, who had a disdain for women (of course, as with most mediumistic information, this cannot be confirmed by any objective means). Nothing conclusive resulted from the night's work, but one resident did report that the threatening atmosphere in the flat had noticeably lightened.

Another private residence was visited on 26 July 2008, although here the owner did not wish the identity of the location to be disclosed. The investigation was prompted by the residents reporting both a sense of presence in the house, and witnessing the movement of

Marischal Street, where East of Scotland Paranormal (ESP) conducted an investigation. (Photo by Geoff Holder)

objects. Because the owners had previously held Ouija Board sessions in the house, which they regarded as successful in some way, ESP cautiously agreed to a request to participate in further Ouija Board sessions.

Generally, responsible paranormal investigation groups eschew the use of Ouija Boards, as the practice has several recorded negative effects. Firstly, it is addictive, often soaking up hours of investigation time (and perhaps can be likened to playing online poker, but with the anticipated payoff being a life-changing breakthrough to the Other Side; like gambling, that paranormal payoff is always just one more try away). Secondly, the very nature of using the board as a collective experience gives rise to what is known as Group Think Phenomenon, where the participants subconsciously or otherwise strive to move the glass or mobile pointer to create the consensus of a meaningful message on the board. And thirdly, the social, intimate personal geography of being grouped around the board means it is easy to infect others with anxiety or paranoia. The story of teenagers being terrified by 'something' after using a Ouija Board is not a cliché for nothing – there are dozens of reported cases, most probably owing their origin to a heightened sense of fear engendered by using the board.

It is also worth stating that many magical practitioners – those who believe in the reality of invisible powers and entities – think that Ouija Boards are actually dangerous. As one modern witch put it to me, 'Playing with a Ouija Board and calling out "Is anybody there?" is the psychic equivalent of leaving your front door open in the middle of a city; you don't know who's going to come through.' Or 'what', presumably (and if it calls itself Captain Howdy, the demon from *The Exorcist*, it is time to end the session *now*). The same individual recommended only using a Ouija Board after setting up magical protection rituals, to ensure that nothing nasty is able to squeeze through the portal that the board presumably opens. There are also hints in the psychological literature that, for a few vulnerable or suggestible individuals, playing with a Ouija Board can unlock some very dark parts of the mind, possibly leading to mental problems.

A low-light photograph taken during the ESP investigation in Marischal Street. This corridor appeared to be the focus of the alleged paranormal activity. (East of Scotland Paranormal)

Two dice, typical of the 'trigger objects' used during paranormal investigations by ESP. (East of Scotland Paranormal)

Knowing that the Ouija Board was at best an unreliable tool, ESP decided to use the occasion to test what kind of conditions were involved when 'messages' were received. First, the group assembled around the board but did not touch the glass or planchette (the wheeled marker often used as an indicator). Perhaps not surprisingly, the glass/planchette did not move on its own, clearly indicating that human participation is required to make it move (and hence supporting the suggestion that the 'messages' spelled out on the board are created by the participants subconsciously manipulating the planchette). They then tried various combinations of the group placing their fingers on the glass/planchette, and rotating the glass/planchette to make it move.

Most of the time the results were vague or nonsensical, but on one occasion the group experiment produced what was supposedly a communication from a five-year-old girl. She spelled out that her name was Gurtt Urquhart, from Aberdeen, and that she had died in 1879 when the ice on a lake gave way. Her brother and a seven-year-old girl had also drowned in the accident, and both were in the room as well. It seemed that Gurtt was not a permanent 'inhabitant' of the house, but visited it on occasion. (Note: I can find no record that 'Gurtt' was ever used as a first name in Britain, but it is possible it is a nickname, a contraction of 'Gertrude'.)

The message caused something of a stir among the group, so a second experiment was decided upon, with a check to eliminate subconscious manipulation of the planchette in search of the correct answer. Each member of the group wrote down a question and, instead of stating it out loud, asked the question in their mind while the paper remained hidden. There were eight questions, of which two were answered correctly. The two-digit number of the house was identified, as was the first letter on the T-Shirt worn by one of the participants. The correct answers were 'visible' in the immediate environment, while those answered wrongly were about the personal information of group members. All of which begs the question of who or what exactly was communicating that evening – was it the spirit of a drowned girl, or an example of Group Think Phenomenon, or was some kind of telepathy involved?

The somnambulist

The following case is not about a ghost as such, but it does have some truly strange features which may throw light on the way psychological factors and altered states of mind may have an impact on the interpretation of apparently supernatural episodes. Dr William Dyce, an Aberdeen physician, was called upon to examine Maria C., a servant girl of around sixteen years of age, who was displaying unexplained, anomalous behaviour. What Dr Dyce discovered was so extraordinary that he wrote up the case in the *Edinburgh Philosophical Transactions*, published by the Royal Society of Edinburgh in 1822. So delicate was the case that Dyce omitted all identifying names and addresses, and the more shocking parts were written in Latin.

The lass suffered frequent 'fits of somnolency', when she would appear to enter into a dream-state or 'an ecstatic paroxysm'. At first, she would appear to nod off in company, but while sleeping she would chatter animatedly about the events of the day, and sing songs and hymns. One evening she said she was at Epsom races, and noisily rode into a room sitting on a kitchen stool, as if on horseback. When in this altered state she could perform daily tasks – such as laying the table, and dressing herself or the children – but did so with her eyes shut. On other occasions the eyelids were only half-closed and, when examined, her pupils were often greatly dilated, not even responding when she was turned to look at the sun. Other times the pupils were very contracted, even in low light. When asked to point out things, she seemed to respond more to the shadow of an item rather than the item itself, and could see outlines more clearly than solid objects. One day she walked and danced on a narrow single plank placed between two vessels on a quay, something everyone said she could not have done in her 'normal' state. She had little education, but in her altered state could read passages aloud or sing hymns with much greater facility than when she was awake.

As soon as she came out of the somnambulist state, Maria could remember nothing that had occurred when she was 'under'. On one occasion, she had attended church in her altered state, and had wept at the sermon (a homily about the wicked life that had recently led three criminals to the gallows). Once herself again, she denied that she had even been in the church, having no memory of the visit. However, during her next paroxysm, she was again asked about the church visit, and clearly repeated the theme and even some of the words of the sermon. Thus it was discovered that, when questioned in her altered state, she could remember everything that had happened in the previous 'ecstatic' episodes; but, in her normal condition, she had no recollection of what she had experienced when she was 'altered'. She described the episodes as arriving with 'a cloudiness before her eyes, and a noise in the head.'

The altered states increased in frequency until they became very common. The symptoms lasted for six months, then ceased altogether when the girl had her first period; but before this something truly awful happened. A fellow servant girl learned that in her normal state, Maria remembered nothing of what went on during her 'fit'. The servant therefore hid a young man in the house, and when the next fit happened the servant girl blocked Maria's mouth with the bed-clothes while her accomplice raped the helpless victim. Maria subsequently had no memory of the assault, and carried on as normal; but during her next episode, she remembered everything and reported it to her mother. We are not told what punishment, if any, was handed down to the malignant duo responsible, and as far as I can tell thereafter the case of Maria C. vanishes from the supernatural literature.

The hauntings of '---- House', in the neighbourhood of the Great Western Road

The title of this case is that used in the original story, as related in the 1912 book, *Scottish Ghost Stories,* by Elliott O'Donnell. O'Donnell had received the tale a few years previously from a Mr Scarfe. Scarfe and his dog Scott spent the night in the allegedly haunted house, which was at the time empty and infested with cockroaches and the occasional rat. Scarfe was a self-confessed psychic and considered the reeking basement to be saturated with the essence of the supernatural. Some kind of presence followed him upstairs, but nothing happened, so the intrepid explorer returned to the basement, despite the fact that Scott refused to budge from the top of the kitchen stairs. Scarfe spent several hours just waiting, then at 2 a.m. the dog came bolting down the stairs and piteously buried its whining head in the man's lap, while the temperature plummeted, the scullery door began to slowly open, and a phosphorescent glow lit up the passage. Scarfe's words give a flavour of the narrative:

'What--what in the name of Heaven should I see? Transfixed with terror, unable to move or utter a sound, I crouched against the wall paralysed, helpless; whilst the door opened wider and wider.'

The glow resolved itself into the figure of a middle-aged servant woman who beckoned Scarfe upstairs. Following her, he watched as she entered a tiny bedroom, pointed to the hearth – and vanished.

The next evening, Scarfe and a friend raised the floorboards and discovered a stamped and addressed envelope. Subsequent enquiries showed that a servant named Anna Webb had hanged herself in the basement when she was accused by her employers of stealing a letter containing money. The missing postal order was, of course, in the envelope that appeared to have slipped between a gap in the floorboards. And thereafter, '—— House', in the neighbourhood of the Great Western Road, was haunted no longer.

Now, it gives me no pleasure to say this, but I suspect the entire story was made up. I cannot prove this, but the circumstantial evidence is suggestive. Elliott O'Donnell (1872–1965) was a prolific author, producing almost forty volumes on the supernatural, plus others on subjects such as crime and murderers. He was flamboyant, cultured, adventurous and exciting. When asked his profession, he replied: 'Ghost-hunter'. He met hundreds of ghosts in America, Britain, and his native Ireland. When I was young, reading his books, I wanted to *be* Elliott O'Donnell

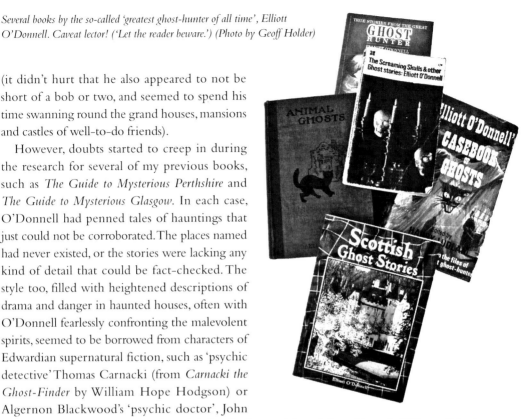

(it didn't hurt that he also appeared to not be short of a bob or two, and seemed to spend his time swanning round the grand houses, mansions and castles of well-to-do friends).

However, doubts started to creep in during the research for several of my previous books, such as *The Guide to Mysterious Perthshire* and *The Guide to Mysterious Glasgow*. In each case, O'Donnell had penned tales of hauntings that just could not be corroborated. The places named had never existed, or the stories were lacking any kind of detail that could be fact-checked. The style too, filled with heightened descriptions of drama and danger in haunted houses, often with O'Donnell fearlessly confronting the malevolent spirits, seemed to be borrowed from characters of Edwardian supernatural fiction, such as 'psychic detective' Thomas Carnacki (from *Carnacki the Ghost-Finder* by William Hope Hodgson) or Algernon Blackwood's 'psychic doctor', John Silence (from *Physician Extraordinary*). I dug further, and found that although O'Donnell had been described as 'the greatest ghost-hunter of all time,' he had also been labelled the 'champion of charlatans'. Even his close friends, such as Peter Underwood, the long-term president of the Ghost Club, could not tell exactly where stood the division between truth and fiction in O'Donnell's work. It seems likely that some of his adventures were true; but which, exactly, it is now too difficult to say. And, when researching his 2008 book *The Haunted North*, Aberdeen author Graeme Milne came to sadly similar conclusions when it came to some of O'Donnell's other Aberdeen stories.

So, although I would like to believe that the great ghost-hunter did indeed meet a man called Scarfe, and that individual did indeed encounter a terrifying but ultimately justified spirit off Great Western Road, I have to conclude that the over-neat story of the 'ghost with a purpose' is simply another exercise of Mr O'Donnell's fertile imagination.

four

OLD ABERDEEN

Focused around St Machar's Cathedral (founded in the twelfth century) and King's College (established in 1495 and now part of the University of Aberdeen), this delightful area south of the River Don still retains something of a medieval atmosphere – but it is no older than 'New' Aberdeen, the main city on the north of the River Dee. In fact, no-one really knows why Old and New Aberdeen are so called. Old Aberdeen was actually an independent town until 1891, when it was finally incorporated into the main metropolis. The street names reflect the area's history, with one thoroughfare bearing the name College Bounds and another called the Chanonry or Canonry, after the canons of the cathedral who occupied manses lining the charming street.

The friendly professor

Given that the area is, in many respects, given over to 'the ivy-clad groves of academe', it makes sense to start with a scholarly ghost. College House, No. 53 College Bounds, was built in the early 1800s and for many decades, up until the mid-twentieth century, it was the home of whoever was then the Professor of Divinity and Biblical Criticism at the university, the house consequently being nicknamed Divinity Manse. Now a private residence for overseas students, its website includes some memories from David and Tom Graham, who lived in the house as children in the 1950s. When the boys' sister was ill, and in her sickbed in the north-west bedroom, she frequently saw a ghost. He was 'a nice man who sat on a rocking chair with a big book on his knee, wearing old-fashioned clothes and rocking and smiling. In this happy house there could only be a friendly ghost.'

Sometime later, Dr Douglas Simpson (1896-1968), the university librarian and a noted author on archaeological subjects, came to visit and asked if anyone had seen the ghost. When the answer was in the affirmative, Simpson described what he expected had been seen – and the description almost exactly matched what the Grahams' sister had witnessed. According to Simpson, the apparition was a former professor who had been due to move into the house, but had died before construction was complete.

More light on this can apparently be thrown from an episode mentioned in Norman Adams' *Haunted Neuk*. From 1919 to 1938, the post of Professor of Biblical Criticism (and consequently

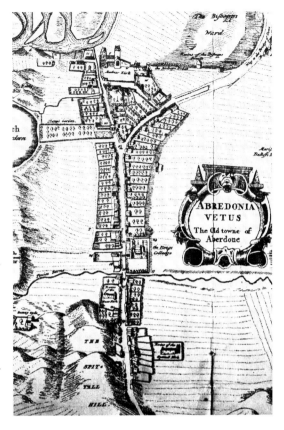

The street plan of Old Aberdeen in 1661, with the cathedral and the River Don to the north. (Author's Collection)

College House) was occupied by Andrew C. Baird. It seems that Mrs Baird had conveyed the details of the case to a lawyer when the Bairds quit the house, and that report reached the Edinburgh Psychic College in 1949 (the Psychic College was a combination of support group for mediums, and a testing ground for psychic phenomena in Scotland; since 1973 it has been called the Edinburgh College of Parapsychology).

The incidents concentrated in the back bedroom (the same room where the Grahams' sister saw the friendly professor). The most common phenomenon was the sound of continuous, heavy breathing, as if from a man in deep sleep. This was experienced by both Mrs Baird's sister-in-law and a nurse, both of whom had disturbed nights as a result. The Bairds' small son refused to sleep in the room unless the door was open, the light on and the family dog present. One night, when all three protections were removed, he screamed out, saying there was a clergyman sitting asleep in the corner of the room, with a book on his lap (remember that Miss Graham had seen 'a nice man who sat on a rocking chair with a big book on his knee, wearing old-fashioned clothes').

Apparently, what happened next is that contact was made with a Revd William Reid of Glasgow, who must have been a spiritualist (or similarly inclined) as he asked his spirit guide to seek out the identity of the mystery ghost. The answer from the Other Side was that it was another former occupant and Professor of Biblical Criticism, David Johnston.

Revd Johnston was minister of Harray and Birsay in Orkney. Born in 1836, he became a professor at Aberdeen in 1893, dying six years later. He seems to have become engaged in some difficulties with the university, probably as a result of his extreme and austere Presbyterian views – he refused to preach in King's College Chapel because it contained that spawn of Satan – a church organ! At some point, the university court asked him to step down, and a substitute professor was appointed. However, irrespective of all this, the spirit of Professor Johnston asked that a message be passed on from him, stating that he was sorry he had frightened people, and simply liked returning to read in the room in which he had enjoyed so many scholarly hours when he was alive. Soon after the investigation in the late 1930s, the phenomena ceased.

A seventeenth-century view of Old Aberdeen, with King's College in the middle and the towers of St Machar's Cathedral in the distance. (Author's Collection)

The medieval buildings of King's College in 1822. (Author's Collection)

The Chanonry, one of the winding medieval streets of Old Aberdeen. (Photo by Geoff Holder)

Ghosts of the Chanonry

William Orem, Town Clerk of Old Aberdeen and author of the 1791 book *A description of the Chanonry, Cathedral, and King's College of Old Aberdeen*, claimed that the sixteenth-century building at No. 12 Chanonry, known as Clatt Manse, had a reputation for being haunted. It was vulgarly known as Tam Framper's house, Tam presumably being the name of the ghost. However, none of this can be checked as the structure, which once stood opposite the west front of St Machar's Cathedral, was demolished in 1644, part of the stonework being used to build the Cromwellian fort at Castlehill, and the rest ending up in George Cruikshank's house at the Bridge of Don.

Novelist Agnes Short wrote a number of historical romances in the 1970s and '80s, although she also penned the creepy short story *Intercom*. For some two decades she lived at Chaplains Court, No. 20 the Chanonry, a delicate medieval survival that incorporates features from a house built here by Bishop Gavin Dunbar in 1519. Before the Reformation, the twenty chaplains from the cathedral ate here around a common table, and, as noted in Norman Adams' *Haunted Neuk*, Short was told by a previous owner that a group of men had been sighted, sitting around a table eating and drinking. Short later picked up other rumours of ghostly happenings in the house from previous years, including sounds of footsteps and the rustling of a skirt heard in a corridor, and the apparition of a seamstress – but the only experience she reported was the sighting of a vague female shape in a bedroom.

Katherine Trail, who was born in College House in the 1860s, and whose father was William Milligan, the first to occupy the chair of Biblical Criticism, recorded her childhood experiences in *Reminiscences of Old Aberdeen*. As a girl, Trail visited one of the former manses on the Chanonry and learned that the house was haunted by the ghost of a young child. Later on, the building was demolished, the workmen finding a curious cache of bones built into the wall behind the fireplace. In contrast to expectations, the bones were not human, but turned out to be game animals such as pheasant, partridge and rabbit.

Spring-Heeled Jack

Mrs Trail also left a record of a more nightmarish ghost from her childhood, the terrifying Spring-Heeled Jack:

A popular Victorian conception of Spring-Heeled Jack, the terror of London. (Fortean Picture Library)

The market cross of Old Aberdeen's cobbled High Street. Supposedly a suffragette's spirit still campaigns in the area. (Photo by Geoff Holder)

I never saw him, nor was I acquainted with anybody who was supposed actually to have set eyes on him, but we children had not the slightest doubt as to his existence. We knew that he haunted the Chanonry at night, enveloped in a white sheet, and jumped over people's heads, and no maid would dream of walking along the Chanonry after darkness had fallen.

This was from an article in the *Press & Journal* on 1 March 1933. Spring-Heeled Jack was an apparently paranormal creature with the supernatural power to leap great heights. He briefly held London in his grip during 1837-8, appearing as some kind of fire-breathing demonic being with burning-red eyes, armour, claws and other horrors. Whatever he or it was, Spring-Heeled Jack entered early Victorian urban folklore and, over the decades, dozens of reports came from cities across Britain, including, as we have seen, Aberdeen, although here there were no actual sightings, just rumours and the kind of terror stories that children tell each other.

Suffragette city

The area has another one of Aberdeen's 'well-known' ghosts whose origin seems now lost in a fog of imprecise memories and urban folklore. Several people have told me of the famous 'suffragette' ghost who has been seen carrying a flag through Old Aberdeen, although no specific details are ever available. She is supposed to walk out of the gateway of a large house near the Bank of Scotland at 91 High Street, and then proceed up the road.

Suffragettes were certainly active in Aberdeen, and members of the direct-action Women's Social & Political Union, the militant but non-violent Women's Freedom League, and the non-militant National Union of Women's Suffrage Societies, could all be found campaigning for women's right to vote in the years before the First World War. A woman carrying a flag does not have to be a suffragette, of course – she could be a trade unionist, or a protestor making a point for or against a political issue – and calling her a suffragette could just be a convenient label that has been applied to the sightings.

Ghosts on the Great Northern Road

Sometime in the nineteenth century, a lady of quality from Hilton House in Hilton was approaching Old Aberdeen, guided by a groom bearing a lantern. At Boathouse Brae, a dark and lonely road with a reputation for footpads and robbers, she apparently encountered an apparition, although no description was given. Boathouse Brae no longer exists, but was close to the old canal (which is now the railway line running through Kittybrewster, between Great Northern Road and Bedford Avenue). The report is in Norman Adams' *Haunted Neuk*.

Of a more recent vintage is a spectre seen by Sean Jessiman, on an autumn morning about 1995, when he was in his mid-thirties and walking four miles every day from his home in Bucksburn to his work at a bakery. Around 2 or 3 a.m., he was passing the petrol station that used to stand at the junction of Printfield Walk and Great Northern Road, when he saw a strange figure clearly visible against the white wall of the garage. It was dressed in a one-piece black cloak and a large-rimmed black hat that Sean described as 'Quaker-style'. No face was visible – it was in shadow or hidden in the black clothing – and the neck was sunken, so that Sean could not even tell if it was a man. He had passed the figure at his usual walking speed, and when he turned round to look at it again nothing could be seen – and there was nowhere it could have gone. He immediately became so scared that he ran the remaining two miles to the bakery, 'and I'm not one for running,' he said to me. This was the only supernatural experience of his life, and it had made a vivid impact upon him. The petrol station has long since been demolished, and is now a block of flats.

Student spooks

Sometime in the early part of first decade of the twenty-first century, an anonymous student living in the Hillhead halls of residence posted a series of strange experiences on a website called The Shadowlands.net. According to the posts, for an entire academic year the student and his/her friends encountered an apparition that persistently appeared in several living quarters at Hillhead, in a laboratory when a class was underway, and even in a nightclub. The figure was described as male, 7ft tall, and wearing a long black coat with a wide-brimmed hat like a Stetson. It would be glimpsed for a second before disappearing, and was frequently witnessed by several people. The student felt that the figure had never actually been alive, but was 'something quite different' to the spirit of a dead person.

On another occasion, the writer of the post was walking from the halls of residence to the campus shop, passing a narrow lane and the part of Seaton Park sloping down to the river, when the student saw 'between six and eight cloaked and hooded black figures'. They appeared to be advancing in a floating fashion through the bushes and grass, although their feet were not actually visible. The witness quickly ran to the shop, then promptly forgot all about the sinister figures, only to see them again on the return journey.

I have no idea what to make of these reports. The tall man in black sounds like the archetype of the super-strong serial killer or supernatural revenge-bent revenant so familiar from horror films, so it would have been interesting to know if the witness was a fan of such movies. Were these sightings symptoms of stress, sleeplessness, malnutrition or some other psycho-physical situation? Or hints of mental illness? Or the scintilla of a hallucinatory or fantasy-prone personality? Or genuine experiences of the paranormal? Of course, the whole thing could be a fiction or a hoax, and as the poster was anonymous, these reports will probably remain forever mysterious.

Equally strange, but better attested, is the haunting of a flat at the Hillhead halls of residence in 2000-1. Each of the six female occupants reported an overwhelming sense of malevolent presence, as if they were being spied upon. Magical practitioner Drennan Gibson, then a science student, investigated the flat and, in his words, 'discovered that a portal had opened in the shower'. A trio of entities had entered the flat through this portal, so Drennan performed a cleansing and banishing ritual, which appeared to do the trick. Certainly all of the women commented that the sense of presence and of being watched had gone. Drennan Gibson is currently the owner of the magical supplies shop Merlin's Grove, on George Street, which was where I heard the story.

Tillydrone Road, the pedestrian route from the Chanonry. To the right is Seaton Park, where a student claimed to have seen several sinister, floating hooded figures. (Photo by Geoff Holder)

Students, out-of-body-experiences, and parapsychology

If you've read this far it will be evident that ghosts cannot simply be explained as the spirits of the dead, and that the world of hauntings is filled with a complex diversity of 'Phenomena Factors'. And in this weird looking-glass world, where nothing may be what it seems to be, there is one Phenomena Factor that is first among equals – the human mind. How we perceive the world, and what goes on among the billions of synapse-firings and chemical reactions within our brain, are important aspects of the 'paranormal'. And never is this more clearly demonstrated than by a series of experiments conducted at the Hillhead halls of residence between 1974 and 1976 – experiments which seemed to replicate some of the ghostly phenomena discussed elsewhere in this book.

At the time, Alistair McIntosh was an undergraduate fascinated by a procedure that seemed to easily and speedily induce what are called 'Altered States of Consciousness', or ASCs. Some kinds of 'lower order' ASC are widely experienced through alcohol or drugs, although here the brain is impaired, possibly even damaged. Non-narcotic ASCs, in contrast, often enhance and improve the mental processes. McIntosh had found the procedure – called, for no obvious or meaningful reason, the Christos Technique – in a book called *Windows of the Mind* written by G.M. Glaskin. The induction process involved laying the subject down, and massaging the feet and then the centre of the forehead, while guiding the individual through a series of visualisation techniques such as asking them to imagine their feet and then the rest of their body expanding like elastic or a balloon. After this, the subject was asked to visualise themselves standing outside their front door, then hovering in the air above the building, and finally imagining that the sun was sinking and they were floating in darkness. All this enabled the person to distance themselves from their body and their usual reality, in preparation for the mental journey ahead.

McIntosh found that 'head music' such as Pink Floyd, the Moody Blues' *In Search of the Lost Chord* and, especially, *Ommadawn* by Mike Oldfield, helped to induce the ASC. He also noted that although half of his subjects were male and half female, the best responders were all women, and the most effective all dreamed in colour, were emotionally sensitive, self-aware and mentally mature, exhibited creative or artistic traits, and had good memories.

Although the Christos Technique had initially been touted as a means of accessing past lives, McIntosh considered that in the experiments he conducted there was no proof of reincarnation. Instead, he categorised his subjects' experiences into three types – lucid dreams, peak experiences and OOBEs (out-of-body experiences). In lucid dreams, the dreamer knows that they are dreaming and remains conscious in the dream – in a sense they have 'dual consciousness', where they are aware of both their dream-world and the real world – so, for example, they could describe to McIntosh what they were seeing and feeling while at the same time fully experiencing the lucid dream. This sometimes produced a powerful dream experience where subjects felt they were living out past lives – for example, one male student, a Communist, found himself as an exploited farm labourer in nineteenth-century Scotland, while a female subject experienced a nightmare where she was a medieval knight brutally killed on a battlefield, but later finding post-mortem peace in a church. In both cases, the subjects thought that either their own experiences and beliefs had influenced the lucid dream, or that they had been subject to the power of suggestion.

In contrast to lucid dreams, which were by far the most common of ASCs reported, peak experiences were the rarest. Here, the subjects described a feeling of joyful oneness with the universe, in which the sense of self dissolved to be replaced by an overwhelming 'super-consciousness' where some kind of bond with the entire natural world was forged. Interestingly, these kind of oceanic experiences have been reported by mystics from across the world's religions and belief systems.

From our point of view, however, the most interesting altered state of consciousness involved a small number of cases where things took a decidedly paranormal turn – the out-of-body experiences. The older name sometimes used for OOBEs is astral travel or astral projection. In one case the subject, 'Ann', not only apparently travelled in spirit to a room on the floor above where the sessions were being conducted, she also accurately reported what was going on there. McIntosh had asked Ann to mentally locate her friend Paula (at this point Ann did not know where Paula was). After a short interval Ann said she had found Paula, who was in her room on the upper floor talking to a girl whom Ann did not know. When asked what perspective she was seeing the scene from, Ann replied that she was floating outside Paula's window, looking in. McIntosh decided to check the information Ann was giving him so he quietly asked Sarah, who was also in the room with him and Ann, to go and check on Paula and describe what she was doing. A short while later Ann, who was still giving a running commentary on what was going on in Paula's room, said someone was coming through the door, started to describe her, and then said in surprise, 'Oh, it's Sarah!' She then added, 'All three of them are killing themselves with laughter. They're in hysterics!'

A short while later Sarah returned not just with Paula, but also with Jill, a girl none of the others had seen before and who perfectly matched the physical description given by Ann of the unknown person in Paula's room. Sarah said that when she had entered the bedroom, she was so amazed by the exact match to Ann's commentary that she had burst out laughing, causing the other two to join in – hence Ann's comment about the three having hysterics. Further investigation revealed several points: Jill had just happened to pop in to see Paula – and McIntosh, Ann and Sarah had no idea she would be there (and had never met her before); and, although it was dark, Paula's curtains were open, apparently allowing Ann's out-of-body spirit to 'look' through the window several storeys high and report on the proceedings. McIntosh concluded that this was a genuine example of an out-of-body experience, where Ann's detached awareness was able to gather information that she could not have known through normal perception, with the part of Ann's consciousness that was still in her body able to provide a running commentary on what her 'other' self was seeing. In other words, it was an authentic paranormal event, here confirmed by several witnesses.

Even more interesting, when Ann was looking through the window from outside, she tried to tap on the glass to attract Paula and Jill's attention. She failed to do this – but what if she had succeeded? Perhaps if she had concentrated more intensely, or had had more practice with her astral body, would Jill and Paula have heard a mysterious noise at the window? Could they even have glimpsed the misty figure of a girl floating outside in the darkness? Could it be that some of the things we regard as 'ghosts' are in fact living people undergoing a temporary out-of-body experience?

Perhaps even weirder than the Ann-Paula-Jill case was the Jill-Iona case. One Saturday afternoon, McIntosh had put Jill 'under' back in Hillhead, and Jill's astral self had decided to go exploring around Aberdeen. She found herself on Union Street, where she saw her friend Iona entering British Home Stores through the automatic doors. Iona, said Jill, was wearing a pink coat and carrying a black bag. Jill's virtual avatar entered the store and watched as Iona spoke to the assistant at the cash desk, took a green jumper out of her bag, and changed it for another jumper on the counter of the same colour but a different style. Jill then saw Iona leave the store at around 4.25 p.m.

Subsequent checking showed that some aspects of this description were entirely accurate, while others were not. Iona had indeed been wearing a pink coat and carrying a black bag, which she did not often use. She had entered the department store on the Saturday afternoon because she wanted to exchange her recently-purchased jumper, and she had spoken to the assistant at the cash desk. But other parts of the description did not accord with reality: she had arrived at 2.30, not 4.25; the store did not have automatic doors; and although BHS accepted the returned garment, Iona had been unable to find a satisfactory replacement and so had left the store and bought another green jumper in a different shop nearby. What the mixture of accuracy and fiction means is hard to guess – are the 'senses' of the astral body somehow clouded by the experience? Or, as with other communications such as radio, does the connection between the astral avatar and the subject become more distorted with distance? (Ann's description of the floor above was spot-on, while Jill's astral voyage to a location some two miles away was beset with inaccuracies.) Whatever the truth, it would be interesting to know whether anyone out shopping on that Saturday in the mid-1970s had experienced anything unusual on Union Street …

The experiments were published in *Worlds Within* by G.M. Glaskin (1978) and *Psychoenergetic Systems Vol. 3* (edited by Professor John Taylor, 1979), while the key points were summarised in *Is Anybody There?* by Stewart Lamont (1980). All these books are now hard to find, but McIntosh's original contributions are fortunately available on his fascinating website, www.AlastairMcIntosh.com.

five

SPIRITS SERVED HERE – GHOSTS OF PUBS, RESTAURANTS & HOTELS

The boss comes back

In May 1973, twenty-two-year-old waitress Agnes McInnes was clearing up after hours in the Cocket Hat pub on North Anderson Drive when she saw a man in the lounge bar, an area that had been deserted seconds before. 'There was a man standing on the floor near one of the pillars,' she said. 'At first I couldn't believe it. The place had been cleared but there was this man standing alone and silent. He was wearing a coat and hat … He looked at me and I was looking at him, but for some reason I couldn't describe his face properly afterwards.' McInnes fetched the licensee, Alex Cormack, but when the two of them returned to the lounge it was empty. Cormack made another check of any possible hiding places and found nothing, although he noted that his dog, which normally came everywhere with him, would not move from his box. Cormack questioned the waitress and realised that her description of the figure exactly matched that of John Walker, the man who built the pub – and who had died in 1959.

When John Walker opened the Cocket Hat in 1955, it was the first new pub in Aberdeen since the Second World War. Its name came from a three-cornered field in the shape of a cocket (a tricorn hat). Alex Cormack had known Walker well. 'He always wore a long coat and a hat with the brim turned up,' he said. 'He had his regular seat at a table on the exact spot where the girl said she saw the man … her description was too close and she was too sincere not to be telling the truth. She would only have been seven or eight when he died and couldn't possibly know what he looked like. It's almost as though the old boss had come back to see how things were going.'

The story was covered in the *Evening Express*, where it was illustrated with what purported to be a photograph of the ghost of Mr Walker standing in the bar. In fact, this was the newspaper's editorial driver – the man whose job it was to drive reporters and photographers to the scene of the action – kitted up in a coat and hat and standing with his back to the camera as a 'stand-in' for the ghost.

Like many such encounters with apparitions, this was a one-off experience and no further sightings were reported; it would have probably never featured in the annals of ghost-lore were it not for the article in the *Express*. Nothing now can be gained from visiting the site – John Walker's pub was demolished and a new Cocket Hat was built on the spot in 1997.

A polt at the Old King's Highway?

The Old King's Highway on The Green is one of the city's longest-established pubs, a hostelry having been opened here as far back as 1741. Parts of the structure are even older, as the basement incorporates part of the Carmelite Friary that stood here until its destruction at the Reformation in 1559-60. The outline of part of the friars' church can be seen in the paving slabs of the car park behind the pub, off Martin Lane and Rennie's Wynd, and the street layout of the area still, in part, reflects the medieval pattern established by the monks. Urban development uncovered human remains around Carmelite Street in 1879, 1904, 1908, 1924 and probably other times before and since, and archaeologists in the 1990s revealed several hundred skeletons from the friary graveyard and church. Monks are popular apparitions, and following the excavations there were reports from the Old King's Highway of the solid-looking figure of an old man wearing a brown or grey cloak; the monkish ghost vanished in seconds.

The first decade of the twenty-first century saw a rash of additional witnessed phenomena, much of it dramatic and spectacular. One member of staff, working in the office at the end of the old basement late at night, saw a pot of paper clips fly off the desk and onto the floor. Another heard their name called out from the recesses of the empty cellar. Strange shadows were seen in the mirrors surrounding the first-floor bar. In the ground-floor bar, a fork jumped out of a glass, and a male and female apparition were reported near the windows at the front of the pub. On another occasion, a customer's mobile phone rang – only the number shown was the phone in the bar, clearly visible to the customer as still sitting on the receiver: she was receiving a call from a phone that was not being used. The call rang out and the group joked that it was the ghost, at which point the lights at the other end of the bar started to flicker.

The apparitions aside, all this is classic poltergeist activity (*see* Chapter Two), something perhaps confirmed by the next incident. One of the staff went up to the first-floor bar to find the room flooded – but the overflowing sink had, until that moment, no water connection to its tap. The tap has not worked since. Elsewhere, a

The Old King's Highway on The Green, site of poltergeist activity. (Photo by Geoff Holder)

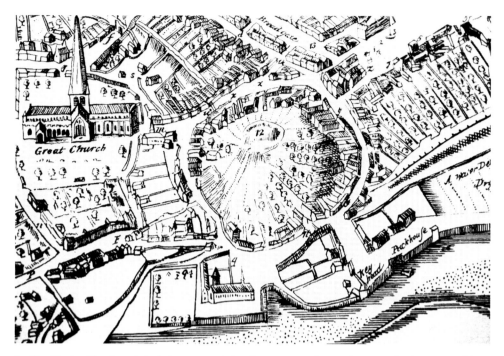

In this 1661 view, The Green is in the lower centre, below the now-removed St Katherine's Hill. The remains of the Carmelite Friary are represented by the small church-like building in the lower part of the map. (Author's Collection)

puddle also mysteriously appeared in the middle of the floor, with no obvious water source nearby. Polts often seem to enjoy introducing water – or fire – into places.

All these reports were collected before East of Scotland Paranormal conducted an investigation at the Old King's Highway on 29 July 2008. With such a range of reported phenomena, expectations were clearly high. As things turned out, the results were mixed. There was a fleeting sighting of a man in a black suit and white collar near the stair area of the basement (could this be the same chap spotted outside the window of Reptiles in The Green, opposite? – *see* Chapter Three). Two female members of the team experienced an unusual sensation, described as a feeling of pressure building up from their legs up to the top half of their bodies or their head. The feeling was sometimes so intense that their eyes would water. The curious thing about this was that none of the men in the area were affected, and the sensation seemed to have a repeating cycle of 2–3 minute periods. Once again, this was in the basement, where further personal experiences included seeing flashes and shadowy figures, and feeling a distinct sense of unease. In the most curious moment, a piece of sticky tape hanging out of reach of the investigators was seen to move rapidly, as if in a breeze, and then slowed to a stop when the team approached. No draught could be felt, and when blown from the mouth, the tape moved a little and then quickly stopped waving, in contrast to the visible slowing down witnessed before.

Although those members of the team who had experienced apparitions and personal sensations in the basement felt there was definitely 'something' there, other investigators encountered nothing substantial. Even worse, none of the alleged phenomena were captured on camera or audiotape. So, while the pub may indeed have unwelcome visitors, the investigation on the night proved inconclusive.

Footsteps at the Four Mile Inn

This pub, on Inverurie Road in Bucksburn, seems to have a minor but persistent paranormal character. The earliest experience I have been able to trace is from the 1970s or '80s, when a member of staff briefly saw a figure dressed as a coachman pass right through a wall. In the 1990s there were several reports of footsteps from locked upstairs rooms. A member of staff with experience of the building told me that from 2002 onwards there had been occasional noises – thumps and sounds of dragging – heard from the same rooms, which are now used for storage but which were once residential. A sense of presence was also sometimes experienced in this area. The same staff member had felt a '1-2-3' pat on her back when she was standing outside the toilet. The only other person in the building was the manager, who was in another room.

A former member of staff reported several events from 2009 – hearing footsteps in the bar when the pub was empty, briefly glimpsing things out of the corner of the eye (most notably a small child sitting on a stool or hiding behind the refrigerator), and, most intriguingly of all, coming out of the office into the bar at 7 a.m. to encounter a patch of white mist at face level. On the other hand, other managers and staff members – one of whom had been at the pub for more than two decades – had nothing to report. If there is something spooky at the Four Mile, it's very subtle.

The hauntings at the Moorings Bar

When Craig 'Flash' Adams bought the Moorings Bar in March 2002, he did not believe in ghosts. 'Can't argue now,' is his current response. For since that date, the building on Trinity Quay has been subject to an astonishing degree of audio, visual and physical phenomena.

The Moorings has been a pub since the 1930s, and in an earlier century the site was a coaching inn – the bar's cellar was once part of the inn, and a claustrophobic and eerie place it is too. These days the bar hosts a number of bands and is decorated with a wide range of rock music paraphernalia, models of skeletons and other weird items. The bar's MySpace site describes its décor as being influenced by 'Every dingy B-Movie bar you've ever seen, including the one in *Star Wars*. And every pirate bar that ever existed.'

The previous owner, John Porter, told Flash that nothing spooky had happened during his incumbency, except perhaps something minor just after he took over in November 1976. But almost as soon as Flash became the owner, strange events began to occur, with the peak period of activity being 2002-5.

Things started in a relatively minor but annoying manner, with interference to the gas cylinders used for carbonating the beer and pumping it out of the kegs in the cellar and up to the bar. If the bar staff want to turn off the beer, the gas needs to be turned a quarter turn clockwise or anti-clockwise – the valve is fairly solid, being too stiff for a child to move.

Yet, several times a night staff working in the bar found that the beer supply had dried up, and on checking found that the barrels were full. In each case, the shut-off valve had been closed. There was no other staff member in the cellar, and any pranksters among the customers would have had to go through the hatch in the bar, go down the stairs and through the cellar hatch, then return the same way, all without being seen in a cramped place with clear sightlines. There was no other access to the cellar.

The interference was a daily occurrence for around two years, firstly with the original pumps in place, and then again when new equipment was fitted in the summer of 2002. After a few months the staff got used to the situation, so when the beer went dry they starting checking the gas cylinder first. At this point, the playful or trickster element of the phenomena first appeared. As if in response to the staff dealing with the cylinder valve, the master switch would be turned off. Again, the staff got used to that and when there was a problem, they went straight to the master switch. Once more there appeared to be a reaction – from then on it was the feed that pumps the products that was turned off. After around 2005, the whole 'switching the beer off' activity seemed to calm down, although there is still the very occasional incident today.

Much more extreme was an episode that took place one summer night in 2002. Craig Adams and Doug Rumbles, the duty manager from 2002-3, were both clearing up after hours. Doug was cleaning tables and Flash was at the other end of the bar. No-one else was in the building. Suddenly there came a sound which Craig described as, 'Rumble, rumble, clunk. Rumble, rumble, clunk. Rumble, rumble.' To their astonishment, both men watched the empty plastic mop bucket move of its own accord. The bucket was the kind with an inbuilt wringer on the top, and had four fixed wheels so there was no cornering ability. It was kept next to the access hatch, under the bar on a plinth. It rolled off this plinth, turned 90°, moved behind the bar floor for perhaps 2ft, rotated 90° again, passed through the hatch, came down off the step onto the bar-room floor, rolled across the floor, stopped halfway between the two stupefied men, and then tipped onto its side and remained still.

Craig mentioned that the phenomena were always at their most intense after closing time. Sometime around three o'clock one morning, a breadknife flew through the gap above a partition wall at the top of the steps to the cellar, and landed at his feet. Craig thought a customer might have been lurking behind the wall, so he walked up the stairs to the bar, but the space was empty. He felt that the knife was not thrown *at* him but *towards* him. In 2003, as part of the renovations, a builder took down the partition wall, working through the night to avoid disrupting the bar's business. The next morning the builder told Craig that the occupant in the flat above had been banging on the floor to complain about the noise. However, only one third of the pub has a flat above it, and the place where he said the noise was coming from was just a flat roof. Craig asked the man to describe the sound, then went downstairs into the cellar and slammed the cellar door, which had a distinctive noise and had often been slammed by the ghost in the recent past. 'That's what I heard,' said the builder. He then realised that he had been at the other end of the bar, perceiving that the noise came from above when in fact it originated from downstairs … which was empty. The builder turned 'white as a sheet'.

On another occasion, a clock flew off a picture hook on the wall and landed on a woman's head, while on several occasions Craig and other members of staff had witnessed glasses jump off the shelf at the far end of the bar and smash. Frank Benzie, the bartender from 2002-9, once saw smoke or vapour rise through the floor by the arcade machine and form itself into a vague shape, before flowing back down into the floor. Staff and customers in the gents' toilet have been tapped on the shoulder by invisible fingers, and heard the sound of sneezing from thin air. And, on one occasion, a Guns'n'Roses tribute band were sleeping in the flat above the pub, having played a gig, when they were all woken and terrified by 'something' in the room with them.

By now the frequency of the phenomena – the door slamming, gas problems, and movement of objects, as well as other incidents such as the fire alarm in the far end of the cellar going off almost every night – had created something of a negative or anxious atmosphere among the staff. It was therefore decided that an investigation should be carried out. Mark Thomas, the bar's sound engineer responsible for maintaining the PA system, told me what happened. Having read up on Electronic Voice Phenomena (EVP), he set up microphones in different parts of the bar after hours, and the staff asked questions out loud, hoping some kind of response would be left on the tape. Around about the second time this was attempted, the recorder picked up a sound which each staff member present attempted to interpret privately. All of them, including Craig and Mark, thought the words were 'Leave the Price List in the Cellar'.

This made no sense to anyone at the time, so they asked around the rest of the team. The only person who could find any meaning in it was Laura Adams, the manager, who was about to clear out a pile of documents and other bits and pieces from the office in the cellar – and among the rubbish was an old price list dating from the 1970s. The price list was duly rescued from impending oblivion and hung on the office wall, where it remains to this day.

On another occasion during an EVP recording, an attempt was made to ascertain the identity of the spirit (or one of them). A list of former employees was read out, and the spirit was asked to make a noise if its name came up. None of the names received a response – except for one, for which a clear tap or click was heard three times in succession, each time the name was repeated. It appeared that the team had made contact with Ted, a barman who had worked for the previous owner. Ted was asked to stop messing about with the gas taps, and thereafter there did appear to be a reduction in the problems. At this point it is germane to repeat the earlier caution about poltergeists – that they have been known to lie.

Mark noticed that on occasion the microphone cables moved of their own accord. Then, one night, as he was setting up the equipment for another after-hours EVP recording, the drums and cymbals started making noises. This was something that did mean something to all those assembled, for that day they had attended the funeral of a regular at the bar – and the man had been a drummer. By using the time-tested but painfully slow method of communicating with spirits – 'If the answer to our question is "yes", please make a noise, if "no", please remain silent' – it was established that they were indeed speaking to their friend. 'Had he been to his funeral?' Yes. 'Had he been to the wake?' No. (Several questions later, the spirit said he had gone to spend time with his mum.)

Mark had the sense that there were several spirits in different parts of the bar, and that they had something they wanted to say. He thought the EVP sessions, by giving the spirits a voice, had somehow cleared the air. By 2005 the phenomena seemed to have calmed down, but there were two unusual incidents to come. One day Mark was in the cellar when he saw a figure enter the office. He went in to chat with the person, but found the room empty – and no-one could have gone back up the stairs without him seeing. On a later occasion, he was describing the figure – dark-haired, stocky, about 5ft 3in tall and wearing a dark woollen jumper – and a regular at the bar said it fitted the description of Ted, the former barman.

Then, sometime between two and three in the morning in 2005, Craig was working in the cellar office when he heard crashing somewhere nearby. As he described it, the atmosphere became very cold, the hairs on the back of his neck stood up, and a passport photograph came fluttering down from the ceiling, landing on the desk face up. Craig's head started to hum, and he felt sick and faint from the pressure. He turned over the picture to find it was inscribed in biro with the word 'Anne' and a date from the 1970s. At this point Craig ran out of the building, and was so scared that it took him many minutes to pluck up the courage to go back in and set the alarm.

Despite the time that had passed since the photograph was obviously taken, Craig recognised it as a woman who was a regular at the bar, but who had not been seen for several weeks. She was well known there, having been drinking at the bar for decades, and had an alcohol problem. Sometime previously, the police had visited, passing round missing person papers for her, but there had been no photograph with them. Much later, author Graeme Milne investigated, and found that the woman had died in hospital, in Aberdeen Royal Infirmary, in May 2005.

Sometime after this incident, Craig tried to find the photograph again, but failed to locate it. He did, however, dig out a box from under the table that contained a very similar image – the one reproduced here. These are Craig's notes on the photo:

The actual photo is passport sized and cut from a strip like you'd get in a photo booth. The back of the photo is dated 30/8/7 and either 7 or 9. Can't make it out, this is in blue biro. This is not the same photo that fluttered down onto my desk, but they are almost certainly from

the same strip. I'm still looking for the other one but have not seen it since that day. The other photo also had writing on the back that said Anne, and a date in the 1970s. Her expression was slightly different in the other photo.

Since 2005 the spirits have been quiescent, and Mark Thomas for one thinks that the atmosphere has improved immeasurably. Occasionally, Craig has been working late in the cellar office and heard footsteps walking back and forth in

This photo of a woman named Anne was found in a box in the bar cellar. It is from the same strip as the image that Craig Adams saw appear from the cellar ceiling. (Craig Adams)

the empty bar upstairs. And on one night in 2009, Craig popped into the loo while a group of four or five staff and friends were hanging around after hours and making their preparations to leave. For perhaps five minutes Craig could hear them clunking about, and he came out asking a question – to find the bar deserted and the door locked, everyone having left immediately after he went to the toilet.

Old Blackfriars

This lovely pub on Castlegate is perhaps a perfect illustration of the way the occasional spooky experience and a historical ambience can be woven into a tapestry of rumour and folklore to create a suggestion that the place is haunted. The atmosphere is particularly suggestive, as the lower part of the split-level pub incorporates the Victorian stained glass, fittings and pews of a former church, and the cosy hostelry abounds in log fires, thick old wooden doors, tables made of recycled timbers, and column-supported decorated ceilings. The word 'Blackfriars' is also redolent of medieval times, but this is a misnomer, as although the land was once owned by the Dominican Friars in the Middle Ages, there was no church or monastery here – in fact, the pub has only been called 'Old Blackfriars' since the mid-1990s. Before that it was Freelands, and prior to that the Royal Oak. (One of the intriguing mementos to be found in the pub is the bell of the battleship HMS *Royal Oak* – not the one sunk at Scapa Flow in 1939, but its predecessor, launched in 1892 and scrapped in 1914; the bell is dated 1889, the year the ship was commissioned.) The pub as it stands now was built in the eighteenth century, and follows the upper slope of Marischal Street as it descends towards the sea. At one point, the upper floor was a location for ladies of negotiable time-based affection.

The Old Blackfriars pub on Castlegate, where a number of spooky experiences have been recorded. (Photo by Geoff Holder)

In terms of unusual experiences, the reports are intriguing but relatively inconclusive. Rachael Hayward of ESP reported that she and other customers had felt a sense of being watched in the ladies' toilet. Around July 2009, the then manager reportedly heard solid footsteps on the floor above when he was down in the cellar: the pub was closed at the time, with no-one else in the building. Barman Stephen Grieve described being on duty in the otherwise empty pub after closing time and hearing the sound of the cellar door slam. Although this door is not on a latch, it is a substantial door and would require a strong wind to move it: the only possible source of a draught would be the back door at the top of the cellar stairs, but this was locked. Also in the cellar, manager Euan Menie several times felt the temperature drop by a few degrees.

Apparently, a spiritualist once claimed that the cellar was haunted by the spirit of a little girl (Mr Menie recalled being told about this haunting by a previous manager when he first came to Old Blackfriars in 1998, but thought it was a story put about to scare the staff). There are also vague tales of children's faces being seen from the cellar windows that open onto the sloping street. Over the years, the legend has gradually grown to suggest that the cellar was used to hold some of the kidnapped children kept for sale as slaves in the eighteenth century (*see* Chapter One for details). This may have indeed been the case, although there is no strong evidence for the claim. So, Old Blackfriars may be haunted. Or it may not be.

The Toast Ghost

In his catalogue of ghosts, *Haunted Scotland*, Norman Adams mentions that in the late 1970s, No. 47 Belmont Street had an outbreak of poltergeist-type activity. At the time it was an office equipment firm, called Typewriter Services and Equipment. The electric kettle and lights would switch themselves on when the power was off and the building locked. Staff would arrive in the morning to find the furniture rearranged, including metal filing cabinets moved clear of the walls and a heavy desk that had moved several feet. The garage door opened by itself and footsteps were heard from an empty room. Typewriter Services and Equipment is now a computer software company with a different name in the West End, but they did not respond to my approach for any further information on the heady days of the 1970s hauntings.

No. 47 was built in the late eighteenth century on what had previously been open pasture running beside the Denburn. Once known as Caberstone House, it was a good quality Georgian townhouse, with two main storeys and an attic and basement. In the 1990s and thereafter, it operated as a social work centre, offering services such as support for victims of domestic abuse. The building has now been converted to a branch of Pizza Express. In December 2009 I spoke to the manager, Caroline Sheils, who confirmed that odd things were still happening – which they put down to the 'Toast Ghost'. Apparently, staff arriving in the morning – long before the cooking equipment was switched on – were often greeted by the distinct smell of toast. Footsteps had been heard on the back stairs when no one was there, and an unlocked filing cabinet had spontaneously locked itself when the key was not even in the building. None of the staff felt that the presence was threatening, and seemed quite fond of the Toast Ghost.

The old-world atmosphere in the lower level of the Old Blackfriars pub. (Photo by Geoff Holder)

The street-level window of the cellar of Old Blackfriars, supposedly haunted by one of the children imprisoned there. (Photo by Geoff Holder)

No. 47 Belmont Street, home of the 'Toast Ghost'. (Photo by Geoff Holder)

The world's greatest medium?

On Tuesday, 22 February 1870, the anonymous 'Local Gossip' column of the *Aberdeen Free Press* published an account of an impromptu séance that had taken place the previous Saturday in the Northern Hotel at 245 Union Street (the hotel caught fire in the 1930s and the block is now shops and offices). The medium was Daniel Dunglas Home, the most famous psychic of the day, an enigmatic individual whose feats baffled scientists and continue to capture the imagination today, even for those who suspect he was basically a master stage magician. Peter Lamont, who wrote a biography of Home entitled *The First Psychic*, called him 'the most interesting man who ever lived'.

On the night in question, Home had been performing as part of a tour, an exercise which did not exploit his psychic talents but which enabled him to use his fame to scrape a living reading other people's works. According to a review in the *Aberdeen Journal* on 23 February, Home had shared a stage at the Saturday Evening Entertainment with Miss Isa Robertson (a sweet-voiced singer) and the Band of the Union ('who played several of their old pieces with the usual acceptance', a damning by faint praise if ever there was one). Home himself had read both humorous and sentimental stories, the best, according to the review, being a piece entitled 'The American Widow'. He got two encores.

So far, so dull, and possibly a bit humiliating for the 'world's greatest medium'. But, back at the hotel things quickly got a lot more interesting. At supper Home was joined by his travelling companion, General Boldero – who was not a spiritualist, but was interested in psychic

The block of 245 Union Street, formerly the Northern Hotel, where D.D. Home conjured up moving furniture. (Photo by Geoff Holder)

An illustration of one of Home's most famous feats, allegedly moving between two rooms by levitating along the outside wall. (Fortean Picture Library)

demonstrations, having previously watched Home perform at a séance in Edinburgh – and several reporters. After warning the gentlemen of the press that nothing might happen, Home appeared to concentrate. Rappings started to be heard around the upper part of the window, or from the cornice, then from the sideboard and upon the table. The *Free Press* description then took a turn to the strange:

> The gentlemen present were invited to look below the table – anywhere, in fact – and nothing was to be seen, but the rapping was distinctly heard. Then they were asked to lift the table, desiring it to be light; and it seemed modestly so, but not to a remarkable degree. Next, they desired it to be heavy, and the very same table, which a few seconds before they had lifted on their fingers with ease, now required such an effort to free it from the carpet that the veins stood out on their foreheads with the exertion made.

After this, a smaller table took to spinning about until it 'collided' with the larger one and could get no further, and a chair advanced a yard or two out of its corner, without any visible agency.

Ultimately the rapping came to the point at which it could be reduced to writing; and the net result rapped out was 'Your-brother-William'; meaning, I presume, that Brother William was present as the rapper.

A report in the July 1889 edition of the *Journal of the Society for Psychical Research*, probably based on an interview with General Boldero, added that 'William' was the name of the dead brother of one of the reporters present, who was deeply moved. The report also added that 'the table quivered so violently and the plates rattled and moved so much that General Boldero states he was obliged to stop eating.' During the séance a large armchair near the fireplace rushed across the room and up to the table, placing itself near one of the reporters at some distance from Home. The reporters, according to the *Free Press*, were on the look out for trickery: 'They were all quite on the alert to discover, if not a spiritual, a material agency, if they could, but failed to do so.' The general also noted that Home had not been into the room until the group all entered it together, 'and no thread or trickery of any kind could have moved the chair with the precision and velocity with which it left its place and abruptly joined them at the table.'

Armchairs rushing across rooms in front of several witnesses was pretty much par for the course for Home. In his most talked-about achievement, he regularly levitated in front of witnesses, once passing out of one window and in through another. He played an accordion in a sealed container through telekinesis, appeared to be able to extend the height of his body, toyed with red-hot coals, conjured up hands without bodies, altered the weight of measured objects, and generally astonished, shocked and bamboozled his fellow Victorians. What really happened that night at the Northern Hotel? As with all Home's other 'miracles' or manifestations, we will almost certainly never know.

Soapy's ghosts

Norwood Hall Hotel is a substantial late-Victorian pile in extensive wooded grounds on Garthdee Road. The wood-panelled corridors conjure up an air of moneyed elegance from a vanished age. It was built (or, more accurately, reconstructed) from an earlier mansion for James Ogston, a 'gentleman capitalist' who made his fortune from Ogston & Tennant's soap factory in the Gallowgate (hence his nickname 'Soapy'). Ogston was also involved in the corps of the Aberdeen Volunteers (an early version of the Territorial Army or Home Guard), joining as a lieutenant in 1866 and retiring as commanding officer and colonel in 1904. He died in 1931.

Ogston seems to have had a complicated personal life. Allegedly, Norwood Hall was actually built for his long-term mistress, while he himself lived with his wife Anne in another large house south of the River Dee. Both women were aware of each other, which must have made for some interesting conversations around the dinner table. It is this love triangle that underlies the identification of the several apparitions that have been reported wandering the dining room, stairs and kitchen. The man is said to be Soapy, while the female spirit is identified as one or other of the two unhappy women in his life. This, at least, is the claim made on the hotel's website. However, enquiries at the hotel produced nothing in the way of checkable facts – such as when the sightings occurred, or what was seen, or by whom – and so there is the possibility that the story has been elaborated to add a sense of frisson for guests.

A second fictional ghost

In Chapter Three, I pointed out that stories which are claimed to be true by the celebrated ghost-hunter Elliott O'Donnell needed to be taken with a pinch of salt. Here is another example. 'The Ghost of the Hindoo Child, or the Hauntings of the White Dove Hotel, near St Swithin's Street, Aberdeen' appeared in O'Donnell's *Scottish Ghost Stories* in 1911. He claimed that it was told to him by a Nurse Mackenzie, an employee of his friend Colonel Malcolmson.

Miss Mackenzie had been working at 'a thoroughly respectable and well-managed establishment,' the White Dove Hotel near St Swithin's Street, where she was engaged as the night nurse for an elderly invalid and former actress named Miss Vining. The patient was apparently suffering from a 'very loathsome Oriental disease'. The hotel building was said to be very old, with thick walls and oak-panelled rooms. Mackenzie felt a terrible gloom in the old woman's apartment: 'I felt it hanging around me like the undeveloped shadow of something singularly hideous and repulsive, and, on my approaching the sick woman, it seemed to thrust itself in my way and force me back.'

Over the next few days, the nurse encountered the apparition of a little girl, her face obscured by a hat. The appearance of the ghost always signalled a worsening in the condition of Miss Vining, and on each occasion the nurse found herself powerless to intervene, as if the ghost could command her movements. Eventually, Miss Mackenzie managed to confront the apparition: 'I snatched at her hat. It melted away in my hands, and, to my unspeakable terror, my undying terror, I looked into the face of a corpse! The corpse of a Hindoo child, with a big, gaping cut in its throat.' At this revelation the nurse fainted, waking to find that her patient had died.

In Miss Vining's belongings, a photograph of the little girl was found, wearing the same clothes she had when a ghost. On the back of it were these words: 'Natalie. May God forgive us both.'

This chilling, superbly-told story has been anthologised many times. However, when author Graeme Milne – another former Elliott O'Donnell enthusiast, now slightly disillusioned – tried to fact-check the story, he drew a blank. There was no record of a White Dove Hotel, or any similar establishment that might have existed but had its name changed by O'Donnell. There was no record of a Miss Vining in the records of deaths kept by the Registrar. In short, it appears that this is another case where Elliott O'Donnell simply made the whole thing up.

six

ALL ABOARD! – TRANSPORT GHOSTS

The Green Lady vanishes

It was December 1956, and John MacDonald of Banchory and his son-in-law Raymond Munro were driving their struggling lorry up the inclines of the A957 Slug Road over the hills from Stonehaven to Banchory. Suddenly, the headlights piercing the wintry gloom picked out a slim woman in a dark green cloak or coat standing on the left roadside. The driver swerved to avoid her and she seemed to draw into herself, as you do when a vehicle comes too close. The lorry braked some ten or fifteen yards from the woman, who proceeded to vanish before both men's eyes. The news report in the *Press & Journal* for 28 December then quoted Mr Hugh Innes of Banchory, who said that the lonely spot was known as the Witch's Well, and was opposite a gully called the Witch's Cave. 'They say that she runs out onto the road and stands there whenever she hears traffic approaching,' said Mr Innes. Apparently, many travellers had seen her, including the late Mr Dow, a coachman of Banchory. Taking a hearse over the Slug Road, Mr Dow's horse suddenly panicked, and at that moment he saw a woman dressed in green, who vanished moments later.

The phantom passenger

The 'Green Lady' story conforms to a well-known theme found in ghost-lore – the 'phantom pedestrian' – with hundreds of examples known from around the world; in many cases the vehicle hits the figure, but no body is ever found. Two related types of worldwide story are the 'vanishing hitchhiker' – where a driver picks someone up who either then vanishes from the back seat, or turns out to have died some time ago – and the 'phantom passenger', in which someone is seen getting onto public transport, but thereafter vanishes. The next tale is an example of the latter.

The form of public transport concerned was one of Aberdeen's famous tramcars; this one was on the Scatterburn line, the period was the Second World War, and the passenger was an elderly woman dressed in black with her face obscured by a hat. As the tram was otherwise empty, and the lady was clearly frail and infirm, conductress Nell Harper helped her onto the vehicle and into a seat on the lower deck. The tram set off on the last journey of the night but, when Nell returned to take the passenger's fare, the woman vanished before her eyes. Nell and George the driver searched the tram, and the short section of track from the last stop, but found nothing.

A common part of 'phantom passenger' experiences is that witnesses start to ponder who the apparition was and why they had appeared. Nell Harper wondered whether the woman was George's mother, who had died a few months earlier. Then, a few weeks later, George himself passed away, and Nell came to the conclusion that the encounter was an omen of George's death. This curious tale can be found in Norman Adams' long out-of-print books *Haunted Scotland* and *Haunted Neuk*.

The omnibus edition

No. 395 King Street, a former barracks converted to civilian use after the First World War, and for decades used as a bus depot, seems to have been the site of a long-term haunting, with sightings going back to the 1920s. A typical report, from the *Press & Journal* for 4 November 1976, described how a driver climbing the stairs on a dark night had recently been 'bowled over' by an invisible force, while when driver John Law was sitting by himself in the staff canteen he felt someone blowing on the back of his neck (the second time this happened the frightened Law took to his heels). A third driver entered the darkened canteen and felt he was not alone. He fumbled his way to the light switch, which did not work, so in panic he too fled – the canteen light only coming on when he reached the bottom of the stairs. The reporter interviewed an anonymous former employee, who said: 'I saw the apparition about ten years ago. It was wearing a three-quarter length coat. It was definitely a uniform.' Five years before this sighting – so around 1961 – the employee was working in the depot at night when one of the office girls came running up to him in a state, saying a man was halfway up the stairs and would not let her pass. 'I went back with her and found nobody there,' said the former employee. 'I am positive no-one else was in the building. It must have been the ghost.' Other reports from the 1970s indicated that bus drivers disliked eating alone in the canteen, cleaners avoided a certain part of the building, and an apparition of a kilted soldier was glimpsed on several occasions.

After the First World War, the barracks building was converted to temporary housing. For his 1998 book *Haunted Scotland*, Norman Adams spoke to Helen Leiper, who told him that on a childhood visit to her mother's aunt in the 1920s, she became bored and wandered upstairs, where she met a soldier sitting on an iron cot in a small room. He was dressed in khaki – but no kilt – and had a bandaged head, while he was winding another bandage round his hands. He stood up – and vanished. Helen went downstairs and told the adults what she had seen, but they dismissed it as childish fantasy. It seems possible that in the post-First World War period the building had a minor reputation for being haunted – many years later, Helen Leiper learned that others had had experiences on the site, and May Cooper, who as a child lived in the former officers' quarters, 'knew' that the ghost lived in the loft. Bringing the phenomena forward into a later decade – possibly the 1950s – was a statement from the anonymous interviewee in the

Press & Journal article from 1976: 'One conductor told me he had seen a ghost when he was a child living across from the King Street garage.'

Graeme Milne took up the case in *The Haunted North* (2008), suggesting that – in classic *Exorcist* fashion – the hauntings restarted in the 1970s when a bus driver used a Ouija Board on the premises (however, as we have seen, there was plenty of activity in the 1960s). Who knows, the driver may have even been inspired by *The Exorcist*, which caused a sensation following its release in 1973 (in the film, the central character uses the board to contact 'Captain Howdy', who is later revealed to be a murderous Assyrian demon).

Milne catalogued some of the recently reported phenomena, including freezing drafts of air and places that seemed unnaturally cold, doors opening and shutting by themselves, the sounds of footsteps or running, and tapping on windows at several different parts of the building, lights switching off and on, and two male voices heard from within a locked shed. For many years the phenomena had been 'explained' as being the spirit of Captain Beaton, supposedly an officer in the Gordon Highlanders who had allegedly hanged himself on the premises. Milne could find no documentary evidence for a Captain Beaton within military records, and suggested that the name was a red herring, having become attached to the hauntings early on – perhaps as long ago as the 1920s – and simply developing a life of its own thereafter, complete with an entirely fictional biography and death.

I contacted Firstgroup, the bus company who now own the depot and are renovating it as part of their new headquarters. Customer Service Agent, Mary Buchan, told me that she had been there for ten years and had experienced no spooky events, and in addition she had spoken to one of the longstanding directors, who also had nothing to report. Without having investigated the site, I am unable to offer any further information, but on first analysis I suggest that the source of the phenomena is not supernatural but environmental. A variety of natural, physical and (possibly mischievous) human causes for the sounds is perhaps being linked to the place's reputation to create the 'haunting'. I suspect there is something in the physical make-up of the Victorian building creating the anomalies – possibly connected to a source of static electricity or infrasound.

Static electricity – the kind that gives you a small shock when you touch a metal doorknob – is a normal, harmless by-product of many things in our environment, such as nylon clothes, or various electrical devices (I'm willing to bet that in the 1970s the bus drivers' uniforms were made of nylon, while the depot carpets were probably also nylon-rich). Small free-floating static electrical charges (ions) build up on your body and discharge when brought near a metal conductor (such as a doorknob). Electrostatic charges can be built up by all kinds of powered devices (as you might get in a bus depot) and sometimes they produce a weird effect called an 'ion wind'. A flow of ions moving over your skin can produce three significant 'spooky' effects – your hairs stand on end, you feel cold even in the absence of any obvious draft, and you have a sensation of being touched. These phenomena match the reports from the canteen.

Recent cutting-edge research by paranormal investigators has shown that infrasound – sound below the level of human hearing – can affect the perceptions and thinking processes of human beings. People exposed to infrasound typically interpret sights and sounds in the normal environment as supernatural, and report feelings of being 'spooked', a sense of not being alone, and threatening atmospheres. Infrasound is often accidentally generated by machinery, piping and ducts – and this *is* a bus depot.

However, even if electrostatic charges and infrasound are factors in the decades-old haunting, and the whole story of 'Captain Beaton' is a wild goose chase, the persistent reports of apparitions over the years remain as impressive testimony.

North Sea spirit

Author James Robertson was told the following tale by a man who had spent many years working on North Sea oil rigs before moving to slightly warmer climes in Trinidad; Robertson, who published the episode in his book *Scottish Ghost Stories*, also received confirmation of the events from two other reliable witnesses. A rig was laid up close to shore with a skeleton crew. One day, when all four men on board were having tea together, the phone rang four times. As this was an internal phone, only callable by someone on board, none of the dumbstruck workers answered. A few nights later, all four were again in the same room when they heard a loud bang outside on deck; investigation revealed no cause. Then the witness started finding things had been moved in his cabin, sometimes to another room. He also had the strong feeling that when he was sleeping someone opened his cabin door and stood looking at him – the feeling was so strong that he had to get up and check the door and corridor, but in each case there was no-one there. The witness never felt afraid or in danger, but he and the others linked the events to the death of a man a few weeks previously – he had been killed while working with sheet metal on the rig.

The 'Phantom Flagman'

We finish this chapter with a story that speaks volumes about credulity, belief, and the thin line between folklore, fable, fact and fiction. The story commences with Queen Victoria on board the royal train from Aberdeen to Ballater, *en route* to Balmoral Castle. As the train sped through the gloaming, she conversed with Prime Minister Benjamin Disraeli about affairs of state. Suddenly the locomotive came to a grinding halt. Puzzled, the Queen sent Disraeli to find out what was going on. The august politician picked his way along the track and found the driver, who was searching the track and said he had seen a figure dancing on the line. No track-trespasser was found, and eventually the observant Disraeli pointed the driver to the headlamp – for on the bulb was a moth, its jitterings being magnified by the powerful beam into a distant figure. Disraeli caught the moth with a handkerchief, and returned to his seat to show the Queen his prize. The royal train set off again, only to be waved down at the next signal box, where it was learned that a tree had fallen across the track further ahead. If the moth had not delayed the journey, the royal train would have passed the signal box before a warning could be relayed, and would have struck the tree, possibly with fatal consequences. The insect was subsequently gifted to the Natural History Museum in London, and can be viewed by anyone who visits there and asks to see 'The Moth That Saved Queen Victoria's Life'.

It's a nice story, appearing in publications as varied as W.B. Herbert's *Railway Ghosts* (1985), Peter Underwood's *Queen Victoria's Other World* (1986), and the *Bulletin of the Amateur Entomologists' Society* (February 2008). It is also completely untrue. I contacted the Natural

History Museum; Martin Honey, the Curator of Macromoths & British Lepidoptera at the Department of Entomology, kindly set out the reality of the matter.

No moth with this provenance was ever donated to the museum, although so widespread is the tale that at one point they had to counter it by having a Departmental Information factsheet for staff to use when explaining the truth to visitors. Most of the enquiries come from America or Canada, probably because the story has appeared in popular ghost books for children there. Martin once received an enquiry from a whole class of children in Alberta, and one American book even tells readers to go to the Natural History Museum where they will see 'the Phantom Flagman', a huge moth displayed in its own glass case. If you look hard enough, the tale even has a pious moral – God sent 'the Phantom Flagman' to save the life of the Queen (or President) – and so is popular with evangelical preachers.

However, there is no moth, no phantom flagman, and no source for the original episode, which sounds like it was invented as a good yarn, an apocryphal story that can be enjoyably repeated to others. In fact, it's so good a story that the details can be transferred elsewhere with just a few adjustments – so the tale is also told in the USA about one of the early Presidents. This is one ghost story that can definitively be put to bed.

seven

PHANTOM ARMIES & RURAL TERRORS

Phantom armies were all the rage in the eighteenth and nineteenth centuries. Spectral armed forces, often consisting of infantry, cavalry and even artillery, were seen in England, Ireland, Silesia, France, Germany, Italy – and of course Scotland. Many pseudo-scientific theories were advanced to explain them, from the *Fata Morgana* (basically, a mirage at a distance) to anomalous atmospheric conditions and collective hallucinations, but many of the sightings remain genuine mysteries.

Aberdeen had several fine examples. The current suburb of Mastrick was once open moorland called White Myres. In the year 1719, a phantom army appeared here not once but twice. At 8 a.m. on a clear, sunny day, around thirty people saw some 7,000 men setting up in battle formation on the moor. The drummers were seen to carry their instruments on their backs, and at one point the long line of soldiers seemed to all topple over, then get up again. After about two hours, an officer on a white horse rode along the line, and the phantom soldiers set off in the direction of Aberdeen, falling out of sight as they passed behind the Stocket Hill.

Another army – or was it the same one? – turned up on the afternoon of 21 October, with 2000 soldiers dressed in blue and white coats, their shining white insignias and muskets clearly visible for three hours in the autumn sunlight. As before, they all fell down at one point, and a commander rode along the line on a white charger before the force marched off (this time in the direction of the Bridge of Dee). A new addition to the sighting was a great puff of smoke, as if they had fired their weapons; but there was no sound of musket-fire. That day a popular fair had taken place in Aberdeen, and in the late afternoon hundreds of people were coming home. In the most amazing part of the whole episode, these pedestrians passed right through the soldiers without seeing them – only when they joined the gaping crowds did they turn around and, to their astonishment, see the army they had just unknowingly walked through.

The two episodes were recorded in November 1719 by Alexander Jaffray, the Laird of Kingswells, although he didn't actually witness the armies himself. He did, however, question a number of eye-witnesses (none of whom he named in his documents, which were much later published in *The Miscellany of the Spalding Club* in 1841). If Jaffray recorded the witnesses accurately, and the people he interviewed were telling the truth, then the Phantom Army of White Myres is one of the great mysteries of Haunted Aberdeen.

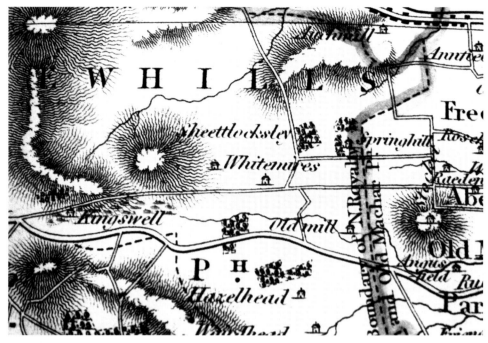

Above *A map from 1822 showing 'Whitemires', where two phantom armies were seen in 1719. Even in the nineteenth century this was still open countryside. (Author's Collection)*

Left *Whitemyres today – a busy industrial estate in western Aberdeen. (Photo by Geoff Holder)*

A slightly less impressive sighting was apparently witnessed upon Brimmond Hill, near what is now Kingswells, at about eight in the morning on 12 February 1643. The tenant of Crabeston farm, William Anderson, reported seeing both cavalry and infantry drawn up, but when the morning mist cleared away, the soldiers also vanished, accompanied by some kind of unusual noise. A certain caution has to be attached to this sighting because it was recorded by John Spalding in his semi-autobiographical narrative, *The History of the Troubles and Memorable Transactions in Scotland: From the Year 1624 to 1645*. Spalding was Aberdeen's first historian, and the book is a valuable account of the awful religious wars, epidemics and other horrors that visited the city in the seventeenth century. But he was also very credulous, and *The History of the Troubles* is chock-a-block with omens, portents, signs and wonders, and cryptic messages from God.

An unusual example of a modern phantom army was witnessed on the Links by the beach, during an idyllic summer's day in 1932. Two lads, George Millar and his brother, had been playing with their grandfather's dog and were taking a rest on the grass. One of them looked up to see a small body of armed men on the ridge of Broad Hill, to the west of where they were lying. The soldiers' bayonets and bandoliers were clearly visible, and some of the men were on horseback. Intrigued, the two boys went up to the spot overlooking Trinity Cemetery, but found no sign of the group, and no evidence on the ground that horses had been there. During their search they asked an old man about the soldiers, and he told them that he had been on the hill for hours and would certainly have seen the men and horses – if they had been there. This intriguing sighting, possibly coloured by the decades since it occurred, but still strange and mysterious, was recounted by George Millar to Norman Adams, who put it in his 1998 book *Haunted Scotland*.

Two rural mysteries

The following two stories came to my attention just as this book was being delivered to the publishers, but they were too good to leave out. The first was communicated by Lyn Western, who noted: 'It was told to me as a young girl by my father, who had to be well-laced with whisky to speak of it!' Lyn's father, Allan Kemp, was born in 1913 at Essie, by Rhynie in north-west Aberdeenshire. One summer night, when he was about seventeen years old, he had been at a dance in Huntly with his girlfriend and, having seen her to her house, started on the fourteen-mile cycle ride back to Rhynie. The moon was bright and visibility was good. As he neared home, he saw a large dog bounding down the field towards him. There had been tales of a dangerous dog on the loose in the neighbourhood, so he was understandably frightened. But, as the hound closed in, a woman suddenly appeared next to the dog and patted its head. She was wearing a long green dress and the style of her clothes suggested the Victorian era. The dog seemed to calm down at her touch, but the now thoroughly-spooked teenager cycled off as fast as his legs would pedal, not looking back.

A few days later, the dog was found dead near the spot where Allan Kemp had seen the lady in green. When he told his experience to his mother – a woman reputed to have been 'fey' or psychic – she was not surprised and said to him, 'Ah weel lad, ye've seen her have ye? She appears to the family in times of need.' Allan, known as 'Mad Kemp', appears to have been a robust individual, surviving several motorbike accidents and breaking nearly every bone in his body, before joining the Royal Artillery and serving in the Second World War as a Desert Rat, and in the Italian campaign; he passed away in the year 2000 at the age of eighty-seven.

The second incident was related to me by Lyn's son, Richard Western. On 21 September 2006, he was on a mountain-biking trip in the Linn of Dee, west of Braemar on the way into the Cairngorms. He stopped at Bob Scott's Bothy, near the River Dee, but the hut was crowded so he camped about 15m from the bothy, close to the river and underneath a tree. It was completely dark by the time the job was done, and it was only then that Richard noticed he had put the tent up in the middle of a 'fairy ring' of mushrooms. He felt a slight superstitious twinge at this, but by now it was too late and he simply went to have a drink with other campers in the bothy.

That night there was a bad storm – the remnant of Hurricane Gordon – and Richard was kept awake by the creaking of the tree above him. Then he heard something else that, he freely confessed, absolutely petrified him. It was the sound of singing, the words indistinct whispers, but the tone that of high-pitched female voices. It was coming from right outside his tent.

For around two hours, the thirty-one-year-old lay in the tent, too scared to even put his head out. He was adamant it was not human singing, or a musical instrument, or an mp3 player or any similar device. Eventually he dropped off, and woke up with the sun shining.

That day he went cycling and later met two women who had also camped close to the river. One was from Aberdeen, the other from Edinburgh, and both were in their mid to late twenties. They spontaneously told Richard that they had heard terrifying high-pitched voices outside their tent, and had spent the night crying and hugging each other. So awful was the experience, in fact, that they had decided to abandon their planned holiday in the Cairngorms, heading instead to Glen Coe. Richard also talked with a Canadian man who had been staying at the bothy for a few days, and who spoke vaguely of having heard 'strange noises'.

Richard, who was brought up in Shropshire but has family in Aberdeenshire, is an experienced outdoorsman and has never encountered anything like this before. Indeed, at a later date he camped at exactly the same spot, and had a perfectly calm night's sleep. The experience is remarkable for being objectively verifiable – at least two people other than Richard separately heard the 'singing'. Perhaps it was some artefact of the storm – or perhaps it was something else. The only thing I can add that might be relevant is that the incident took place on the Autumn Equinox. In *The Secret Commonwealth*, the strange manuscript on the realm of Faery (written by the Revd Robert Kirk, the seventeenth-century Episcopalian minister of Aberfoyle), the Quarter Days, as the Equinoxes and Solstices are called, are said to be especially significant. For it was on these dates that the Sidhe (the fairies) travelled abroad, and those who were 'fey' were in danger of inadvertently encountering the fairy host.

APPENDIX – ACCESS TO LOCATIONS

Some of the locations featured in this book are open to the public, including:

The Tolbooth Museum of Civic History
Entrance on Castle Street, next door to Lodge Walk. Typically open July – September, Tuesday – Saturday, 10 a.m. – 5 p.m. (closed for lunch), and Sunday 12.30 p.m. – 3.30 p.m. Check www.aberdeencity.gov.uk for exact times. Admission free. Numerous stairs, with wheelchair access only to the entrance area on the ground floor, and not to any of the cells or rooms (a video 'virtual tour' is available). Frequent themed events.

Provost Skene's House
Entrance off Flourmill Lane or Broad Street. Open Monday – Saturday, 10 a.m. – 5 p.m., closed Sunday. Admission free. Guidebook available. Disabled access only to café on the ground floor, within the vaulted former cellar.

His Majesty's Theatre
Rosemount Viaduct. Open from 9.30 a.m. Monday – Saturday, closing times vary depending on show times. Bars/restaurant. Full disabled access.

Central Library
Rosemount Viaduct. Open 9 a.m. – 5 p.m. Tuesday, Thursday, Friday and Saturday, 9 a.m. – 8 p.m. Monday and Wednesday. Café. Disabled access to all floors.

Aberdeen Arts Centre
31 King Street. Normally open Monday – Saturday, 10 a.m. – 4 p.m. and, in the evenings, 45 minutes before performances. Café/bar. Disabled access to the downstairs rooms and the theatre.

Other
The shops, markets, pubs, restaurants and hotels mentioned all welcome customers. Most of the other locations mentioned are not open to the public: please respect the owners' privacy.

SELECT BIBLIOGRAPHY

Abercrombie, John, *Inquiries Concerning the Intellectual Powers and the Investigation of Truth* (Waugh and Innes, Edinburgh; John Murray, Edinburgh; and Whittaker & Co., London, 1835)

Adams, Norman, *Haunted Neuk: Ghosts of Aberdeen and Beyond* (Tolbooth Books, Banchory, 1994)

——————— *Haunted Scotland* (Mainstream Publishing, Edinburgh, 1998)

——————— *Blood and Granite: True Crime from Aberdeen* (Black & White Publishing, Edinburgh, 2003)

——————— *Hangman's Brae: True Crime and Punishment in Aberdeen and the North-East* (Black & White Publishing, Edinburgh, 2005)

Brown, Chris, *The Battle of Aberdeen 1644* (Tempus, Stroud, 2002)

Crowe, Catherine, *The Night Side of Nature, or, Ghosts and Ghost-Seers* (T.C. Newby, London, 1848)

Cutten, George Barton, *Three Thousand Years of Mental Healing* (Charles Scribner & Sons, New York, 1911)

Davies, Owen, *The Haunted: A Social History of Ghosts* (Palgrave MacMillan, Basingstoke and New York, 2007)

Grant, James, *The Mysteries of All Nations* (W. Paterson, Edinburgh; and Simpkin, Marshall, & Co., London, 1880)

Gurney, Edmund, Frederic W.H. Myers & Frank Podmore, *Phantasms of the Living* (The Society for Psychical Research/Trubner & Co., London, 1886)

Halliday, Ron, *Evil Scotland* (Fort Publishing, Ayr, 2003)

Herbert, W.B., *Railway Ghosts* (David & Charles, Newton Abbot & London, 1985)

Holder, Geoff, *The Guide to Mysterious Aberdeen* (The History Press, Stroud, 2010)

Kennedy, William, *Annals of Aberdeen* (A. Brown & Co., Aberdeen; W. Blackwood, Edinburgh; and Longman *et al*, London, 1818)

Lamont, Stewart, *Is Anybody There?* (Mainstream Publishing, Edinburgh, 1980)

Lee, Frederick George (ed.), *Glimpses of the Supernatural* (Henry S. King and Co., London, 1875)

Lindley, Charles, Viscount Halifax, *Lord Halifax's Ghost Book* (Geoffrey Bles, London, 1953 – first published 1936)

Love, Dane, *Scottish Spectres* (Robert Hale, London, 2001)

McIntosh, Alastair, 'A Commentary on the "Christos" Technique' (1978) and 'The "Christos" Procedure: a Novel ASC Induction Technique' (1979), both from www.AlastairMcIntosh.com

Macnish, Robert, *The Philosophy of Sleep* (D. Appleton, New York, 1834)

Milne, Graeme, *The Haunted North: Paranormal Tales from Aberdeen and the North East* (Cauliay Publishing, Aberdeen, 2008)

Moss, Peter, *Ghosts Over Britain* (Elm Tree Books, London, 1977)

O'Donnell, Elliott, *Scottish Ghost Stories* (Kegan Paul, Trench, Truebner & Co., London, 1911)

Orem, William, *A Description of the Chanonry, Cathedral, and King's College of Old Aberdeen, in the Years 1724 and 1725* (J. Chalmers and Co., Aberdeen, 1791)

Prichard, James Cowles, *A Treatise on Insanity and Other Disorders Affecting the Mind* (Sherwood, Gilbert and Piper, London, 1835)

Rannachan, Tom, *Psychic Scotland* (Black & White Publishing, Edinburgh, 2007)

Robertson, James, *Scottish Ghost Stories* (Warner Books, London, 1996)

Society for Psychical Research, *Journal of the Society for Psychical Research Volume 6* (1893-94)

Spalding, John, *The History of the Troubles and Memorable Transactions in Scotland: From the Year 1624 to 1645* (T. Evans, London, 1792)

Swan, Edi, *His Majesty's Theatre: One Hundred Years of Glorious Damnation* (Black & White Publishing, Edinburgh, 2006)

Trail, Katherine E., *Reminiscences of Old Aberdeen* (D. Wylie & Sons, Aberdeen, 1932)

Upton, Bernard, *The Mediumship of Helen Hughes* (Spiritualist Press Ltd, 1945)

East of Scotland Paranormal: www.esparanormal.org.uk

INDEX